Mulan
and the
Modern Controversy

The Unconquerable Spirit
of a Young and Courageous
Chinese Warrior Woman

Also by this author

Nat Turner's Holy War To Destroy Slavery
America's Female Buffalo Soldier: Cathy Williams
Miller Cornfield at Antietam
Pickett's Charge
Death at the Little Bighorn
Barksdale's Charge
Storming Little Round Top
Exodus From The Alamo
Emily D. West and the "Yellow Rose of Texas" Myth
The South's Finest
George Washington's Surprise Attack
How The Irish Won The American Revolution
Why Custer Was Never Warned
The Alamo's Forgotten Defenders
Irish Confederates
God Help The Irish!
Burnside's Bridge
The Final Fury
Westerners In Gray
Alexander Hamilton's Revolution
The Confederacy's Fighting Chaplain
Cubans In The Confederacy
Forgotten Stonewall of the West
From Auction Block To Glory
The Important Role of the Irish in the American Revolution
The 1862 Plot to Kidnap Jefferson Davis.
Anne Bonny: The Infamous Female Pirate
America's Forgotten First War for Slavery and Genesis of The Alamo
For Honor, Country, and God: Los Niños Héroes
Targeting Abraham: The Forgotten 1865 Plot To Assassinate Lincoln
A New Look at the Buffalo Soldier Experience in Wartime Vol I:
Corporal David Fagen's Metamorphosis and Odyssey
Nanny's War to Destroy Slavery
The Irish at Gettysburg
Blacks in Gray Uniforms
Glory At Fort Wagner: The 54th Massachusetts Vol I
Martyred Lieutenant Sanité Bélair
Gran Toya: Founding Mother of Haiti
Claudette Colvin: Forgotten Mother of the Civil Rights Movement

Mulan
and the
Modern Controversy

The Unconquerable Spirit
of a Young and Courageous
Chinese Warrior Woman

Phillip Thomas Tucker, Ph.D.

ISBN: 9798695691771

PublishNation LLC
www.publishnation.net

Contents

Chapter I

Genesis of a Legend

More than 1,500 years ago, a young Chinese girl from north China named Mulan overturned the traditions and conventions of her strict patriarchal society because she loved her father and her people of north China. In the process, she created an enduring and beloved ancient Chinese legend that has continued to be cherished to this day by becoming a courageous warrior disguised as a male and performing heroically on numerous battlefields.

After all, this period was at a time in ancient China when women were thought to have been worthy as only serving as concubines and child bearers in an ancient male-dominated world of her northern nomadic society of the Northern Wei Dynasty.

Dressing like a male warrior with her long black hair tied-up under her war helmet and with her feminine figure hid by a suit of body armor that had been once worn in battle by her beloved father, Mulan successfully disguised her sex to serve in the army for more than a decade. Year after year, she fought as a highly-skilled warrior of distinction on the battlefield in defense of her nomadic people of the north and her beloved homeland: an enduring example of courage, patriotism, and noble self-sacrifice to the Chinese people for centuries.

Even more and most important, Mulan systematically shattered the dominant negative stereotypes that women were so weak and helpless that they were destined by God and nature to be autocratically ruled by men, as if they were nothing more than overgrown children in the traditional patriarchal view that dominated Chinese society.

But fact, the complete submission of Chinese women was nothing more than a myth long embraced by the West in one of the most pervasive stereotypes. In truth and as realized by the Chinese people and as Mulan's case fully demonstrated, Chinese women often mocked the most common of negative western stereotypes by their own initiative and bold actions just like women in other lands.

To answer the urgent demand for one soldier to serve in the army from each family by the imperial court of the Khan, who ruled her nomadic society, which meant her father, an aged war veteran, would have to serve in the army to meet the threat of foreign invaders, Mulan took immediate action. She boldly decided to serve as a soldier in place of her old and crippled father. She knew that her disabled father would surely die if he went to war in his feeble condition because the upcoming campaign was guaranteed to be long and hard.

For such reasons, the popular folk legend of Mulan came to be viewed as the ideal example and model of the perfect filial daughter by the Chinese people for centuries. She saved her father's and family's honor by serving for years with distinction on the battlefield, while conforming to the central values of Confucian ethics and moral principles of ancient China, especially loyalty to family, God, ancestors, and her people, who she defended with her life on multiple fields of strife.

Therefore, Mulan's years of military service, in which she demonstrated her equestrian skills while riding her war horse and mastery of the "bending of the bow" and other weapons of choice, was basically an act of noble self-sacrifice that saved her family's honor and her father's life in the end. And this honor could only be gained by Mulan risking her life on the battlefield in fighting the invaders of her homeland for more than a decade: a classic example of the time-honored Confucian concept of filial piety.

These admirable qualities of this young Chinese woman, who had been raised on strict Confucian ethical values, have explained why the legend of Mulan has been so revered and why she had been idolized as a national heroine and heroic model by the Chinese people for centuries. In the process of becoming a warrior of rare distinction in battling the "barbarian" invaders, who had descended from the north, of her homeland, Mulan not only won distinction but also gained an unprecedented personal sense of freedom and mobility that were unknown to the other women of her strict patriarchal society of northern nomads.

Consequently, Mulan became the most popular Chinese folk heroine of an ancient culture thousands of years old and like no other woman in the annals of Chinese history in what was nothing less than a cultural phenomenon second to none in the annals of Chinese folk history. All the while confirming to the most cherished and respected Confucian values of her ancient society, Mulan shattered a plethora of anti-women stereotypes and overturned societal prejudices that had long belittled women as nothing more than objects in an oppressive male world, which she also symbolically fought against like the enemies of her northern homeland.

A key part to its overall appeal for centuries to people of all classes and ages in China, the enduring legend of Mulan has thoroughly shattered the western stereotypical view of Chinese women having been perpetually the victims of a powerful traditional patriarchy of China. As known by the Chinese people, the fundamental truths of Chinese life and history were in fact far more complex than have been long assumed by westerners, defying the simplistic stereotypes of the West about the Chinese: ignorance born of the longtime wide disconnect between East and West.

The story of Mulan is one of the most classic works in the annals of ancient Chinese history because of its immense popularity among the Chinese people over the course of centuries and its popularity among the common people of this ancient nation has never diminished.

Ironically, the beginning of the written legend of Mulan could not have been more obscure or shadowy, however. The legend of Mulan first appeared in written form of only around 300 words from the hand of an unknown writer as folk ballad—a heroic narrative poem entitled "Mulan shi": "The Ballad of Mulan" that was undated and extremely non-specific in regard to basic details about Mulan's life.

This ancient poem was first penned in a setting in the north of China at some point between the fourth and sixth centuries during the Northern Wei Dynasty (386-534).

The little existing evidence has revealed that the thirteenth century was the time that Mulan performed her stirring exploits on battlefields in the north during a time of trouble for her people. However and as mentioned, it was not until the famous poem's creation—in its first written form which was extremely vague—that the legend of Mulan was written down at some point by the unknown Chinese author between the fourth and sixth centuries.

Like so much about the popular Mulan legend, the inherent contradictions and discrepancies about this ancient poem called "The Ballad of Mulan" and its creation have abounded to an extraordinary extent. For such reasons, the story of Mulan has continued to be almost continuously reinterpreted, shaped, and reworked for generations, including today and especially in the West.

Significantly, the ancient poem, or "ballad," emphasized that Mulan served the Kahn instead of the Chinese emperor of the Han people, who were the majority of Chinese: evidence that has revealed a great deal about the ballad's roots among the nomadic tribes of north China situated south of the Mongolia border. However, like the exact location of the poem's setting and the original author's name, Mulan's exact ethnicity was not revealed in the frustratingly short folk ballad known simply as "The Ballad of Mulan."

However, to leading Chinese scholars, the word Kahn and other revealing words have partly indicated that Mulan was most likely part of an ethnic group of the Xianbei people (also known as the Sienpi) of the Northern Wei Dynasty of northeastern China and that she engaged in the conflicts that were waged in that northern region, when raiders from Mongolia struck south into northern China.

Contrary to the common stereotype that she was a Han Chinese which was China's dominant ethnic group both then and today, Mulan's ethnicity was that of the Tuoba people. The Tuoba were members of a nomadic clan in the north that consisted of the Xianbei people, who were a non-Han group. As noted, the Han people dominated the rest of the vast expanse of China except in the north along the border with Mongolia to the north.

Likewise in still another significant omission in a surprising development, the ancient poem written centuries ago failed to name the exact identities of the enemies of Mulan's people, which has become another factor that has surrounded the famous ballad in mysteries and controversies that exist to this day.

However, as noted, this obscurity was no stranger than the somewhat unsettling reality that the Chinese author of "The Ballad of Mulan" is entirely unknown to this day. Because this most famous ancient folk tale of Chinese history was written from the hand of an unknown author, this unfortunate situation has only allowed generations of latter-day writers to fill in the extensive gaps in Mulan's story with endless embellishments and exaggerations.

The anonymous quality that has surrounded "The Ballad of Mulan"—China's most famous ancient story—like a shroud from the beginning was quite unlike the West's earliest most famous ancient story that also began as an unwritten folk ballad. This song had been long sung to ancient Greek audiences like the "Ballad of Mulan" had been sung to ancient Chinese audiences, Homer's *Iliad*.

Even more, the legendary "The Ballad of Mulan" failed to explain the exact nature of Mulan's military exploits or even her family background—a glaring blank canvas that has continued to be filled-in by imaginative Chinese, and then Western, writers, historians, and filmmakers and most recently by the Disney Company in early September 2020 with the release of the full-length feature film *Mulan*.

Regardless of the many discrepancies and striking omissions in the historical record that exist in regard to Mulan's story from this anonymous writer who evidently possessed scant exact details about this warrior woman, millions of people around the world have closely embraced the inspirational legacy of Mulan as a model of courage, devotion to duty and family, and love of country.

Basically, over an extensive period of time, two distinct Mulan's have developed and have persisted to this day: the real person and the mythical person that was mostly created in the twentieth century and the twenty-first century. During the twentieth century, the very existence of the Chinese government and the life of the Chinese nation were at stake when imperial Japan invaded China in the summer of 1937. Consequently, a national heroine was needed by the beleaguered government to inspire the people during the invasion by Japanese forces in the Second Sino-Japanese War, which was basically the beginning of the Second World War.

To bolster the war effort and raise the morale among the people, an authentic Chinese heroine was required by the central government to inspire the Chinese people to greater exertions because of the success of the Japanese invasion against a far weaker opponent. Significantly during the invasion of their homeland, large numbers of Chinese women served in the ranks and fought against the invading Japanese, when the heroic story of Mulan was still on their minds: an enduring inspirational legacy not lost to large numbers of these modern Chinese women warriors.

The horrors inflicted by the Japanese invaders were most forcefully demonstrated during the massacre of tens of thousands of civilians and the destruction at Nanking in late 1937 and early 1938: one of the greatest tragedies of the Second World War, which was popularized by Chinese-American historian Iris Chang in 1997 in her award-winning book *The Rape of Nanking*.

However, the mythical Mulan has been created by generations of Chinese writers, historians, poets, artists, and filmmakers long before the Second World War and then the belated entry of the Disney Company, beginning during the last years of the twentieth century, in celebrating the fascinating story of Mulan. Unfortunately, of course, the real Mulan has never told her story in her own written words, because "The Ballad of Mulan" was first written by an anonymous writer long after her death. Consequently, the original words of Mulan have been lost forever because her tale has only survived in popular legend and folklore for centuries.

Therefore, as noted, this short ancient folk tale, "The Ballad of Mulan," of less than 310 words has been the single source of Mulan's story and it came from a mysterious and unknown source: an exceedingly brief and scant amount of secondary historical evidence that has grown into the most enduring and famous ancient Chinese legend in history in what has been a remarkable transformation.

Indeed, "The Ballad of Mulan" became a permanent part of classic Chinese literature that has always been popular among the people of China, while having evolved into a cultural icon beloved by the Chinese people. For her loyalty, self-sacrifice, patriotism, and courage that she demonstrated in battling for her family, people, and Khan, Mulan became enshrined as a Chinese heroine second to none based upon the 300-word poem from an unknown writer and without any collaborating evidence whatsoever from the same time period: a rather remarkable development that has been unprecedented in regard to the stories of heroines around the world.

Like no other folk heroine, which has included a lengthy cast of warrior women throughout the course of Chinese history, the inspiring story of Mulan has embodied some of the most noble traits of the Chinese people, who had long struggled against all manner of adversity, especially from seemingly countless foreign invaders to eventually become a nation.

China had early evolved into one of the world's great civilizations when the West was still enveloped in the backwardness of the Dark Ages. Indeed, the legend of Mulan has been long warmly embraced by the people of China at a time when their civilization far outshined any societies that existed in the West at the time, which were extremely primitive by comparison.

Embracing a means of personal empowerment when the opportunity presented itself with the call to arms from the Kahn, Mulan made a bold decision that defied Chinese traditions, customs, and all expectations of women by performing her duty on the field of strife during years of hard campaigning: a popular folk tale of ancient China, which has captivated both the Eastern and Western worlds to this day.

When the ruling court of the Kahn issued orders for her infirm and aged father to join the Xianbei's people's army of the Tuoba clan of the Northern Wei Dynasty for a new campaign against the hard-hitting raids launched south by an aggressive Mongol-related people, the Rouran (also known as the Ruru) of the Rouran Khaganate, according to at least one leading historian, Mulan finally came into her own. These raiders struck the north of China from the seemingly endless steppes located in the depths of Inner Mongolia.

For this reason, Mulan boldly stepped forward in the place of her disabled father to meet the demands of the Khan and the ominous threat from the north. The overall situation was critical because the "barbarian" raids had slashed deeply into the lands and settlements of Mulan's people, who were members of the Northern Wei Dynasty, to the south.

The powerful Rouran Khaganate of the eastern steppe of today's Mongolia consisted of a confederation of nomadic tribes that was composed of people of a proto-Mongolic origin. This aggressive group rose to prominence during the late fourth century to the middle of the sixth century. The Rouran were eventually defeated by the First Turkic Khaganate (522 to 744) and long before the rise of Genghis Khan and the so-called Golden Horde of the Mongol Empire in the twelfth century.

As mentioned, ironically, the original written story— "The Ballad of Mulan"—about Mulan failed to mention the identity of her enemies. However, the Northern Wei Dynasty had been long under threat of the invaders from the north. Ancient Chinese texts have described these raiders from today's Mongolia simply as "barbarians," which applied to any foreign people, especially westerners, who were not Chinese. It was members of these proto-Mongolic tribes who came from the depths of the eastern steppes of Mongolia and raided south into northern China to cause destruction among the people of the Northern Wei Dynasty.

Long before the rise of Genghis Khan who conquered large stretches of territory stretching from Europe to Asia to create a vast empire and until it seemed that he and his Mongol warriors were invincible and as mentioned, these threats to Mulan's people, who were also nomads, stemmed from this proto-Mongolic people. These nomads were expert warriors who hailed from the vast lands of mountains, deserts, and steppes that were nestled between Russia to the north and China to the south—modern Mongolia.

For an extended period of time, these fierce raiders posed a severe threat to Mulan's nomadic non-Han people, who were ruled by their Khan. Consequently, the Kahn needed every possible fighter (one per family that included either the father or son to thwart the escalating threat from the north), when the crisis was at its height. Basically,

Mulan served as a substitute for her father in the army, almost as if she was her father's son, while battling for the family's and people's honor.

Indeed, and as noted, to keep her aged and infirm father from serving in the army that would have been a certain death sentence for the old warrior, Mulan finally came into own as a woman warrior of distinction, while wearing her father's suit of armor and fighting beside male warriors, who never knew that she was a female. In her clever disguise of a male that gave no hint of her true sex, she bravely answered the call of the Kahn who ruled her nomadic people of the North Wei Dynasty when they faced the growing threat from Mongolia, after having made the decision on her own and even when family members had attempted to dissuade her.

All in all, Mulan's own personal choice of going to war was an example of noble self-sacrifice by this remarkable young woman. When she risked her life to serve as her father's son as a substitute in the army because of his old age and infirmities, this allowed her father, an army veteran, to remain at home to provide for the family that badly-needed his presence and assistance.

In this sense, Mulan was primarily motivated by love of family while her duty of serving the Khan was secondary, because the family always came first, especially when in times of need and crisis: contrary to modern interpretations of the Chinese Communist state, which always comes first in the lives of its people, that has often employed the legend of Mulan to rally support and obedience, especially in wartime, among the people around the dictates of the central government.

When the time came, Mulan was fully and well prepared for the formidable wartime challenge because of her early interest in her father's military service and the overall development of her own martial skills at an early age. After donning her father's suit of armor and mounting a warhorse with all the wartime gear weapons, such as sword, spear, and bow and arrows, that were necessary for effective warfighting against the so-called "barbarians" from the north, Mulan had decided to do what was most honorable, but entirely unheard of for a female: the courageous act of fighting against the enemies of her people and in defense of her beloved homeland.

Displaying her deep sense of patriotism and self-sacrifice to an imaginable degree for a woman of her day when the expectations for a young female were centered exclusively on motherhood and being a good wife at home, Mulan then served as a brave frontline fighter for more than a decade. Performing what she believed was her sacred duty for a dozen years according to "The Ballad of Mulan," Mulan battled for her family's and people's honor on distant battlefields of her threatened homeland. She won distinction and widespread recognition for her martial prowess and heroics, including the gaining of considerable renown in the imperial court of the Kahn, who never suspected her true sex.

In the process and as noted, Mulan became a revered heroine second to none and legend that has thrived for centuries in China, before only becoming first known in the western world by way of an English translation of "The Ballad of Mulan" that appeared in the nineteenth century. For the first time, westerners then learned about Mulan who remained an obscure and little-known figure in the West. Therefore, unlike in China, the popularity of story of Mulan in the West has been a relatively recent development, but its overall appeal has become nearly as strong and timeless in the West than in the East by the twenty-first century.

In the process of refusing to accept the traditional lowly and subservient domestic role assigned to her by her patriarchal society and one that was expected of her since her birth, Mulan relied on her wits and intelligence to escape the restrictive bonds of her world to empower herself and gain her personal freedom with the gaining of a new identity—the skilled and respected female warrior who fought in the disguise of a male.

In this way, Mulan became precisely what was most socially esteemed and valued in ancient Chinese society, which was not only a male warrior identity of a proud defender of her scared north China homeland and her people in wartime, but also a heroic status that lifted her higher up the ladder of the social order, despite having been a female which continued to be her great secret year after year: an unprecedented development for a young woman at a time when it was unthinkable for a woman to boldly step foot into the warrior world, which had been an exclusive male domain since time immemorial, and excel to a remarkable degree.

As a dynamic woman warrior who won distinction on the battlefield and who gained a leadership status in wartime while in charge of large numbers of male fighters and leading them into battle, Mulan excelled in the wartime environment by mastering the warfighting and leadership skills that exceeded those abilities of so many of her male comrades.

Most important by having gone to war in an audacious decision that she never regretted except in missing her family in her long absence from home of more than a decade, she succeeded in escaping the lowly domestic and subservient expectations—almost a slave-like status and the traditional position of a good wife whose main function in life was to bear children, which was the highest status for a woman in ancient Chinese society—and a traditional powerlessness for women imposed by men that had long reduced them to objects for decoration or sex.

Most of all, Mulan proved that nothing was impossible and out-of-reach for a determined young woman of courage and character in times of crisis, when such sterling qualities were called for and demanded by the Khan: a timeless tale about a lowly female rising up to seize her own destiny and achieving great things on her own by way of her own God-given abilities and talents.

Seemingly countless generations of the Chinese people have been raised on the inspirational story of Mulan, which has provided an enduring lesson about the importance of courage, devotion to family, and the love for the sacred homeland in which they had been born. Above all and far more than for herself, Mulan only desired to do what was best for her family and homeland that she loved with a passion.

And in the Confucian tradition, this sacred duty to the family, Kahn, and her people and homeland meant facing ancient enemies—battle-hardened raiders who rode like the wind on horseback and who were expects in the deadly art of swordsmanship and firing with a bow and arrow from the saddle while rapidly on the move—on the field of strife for years at a time when the idea of women warriors was an inconceivable concept to the male fighters, who she served beside and led into battle year after year.

Over the course of centuries, Mulan became an enduring Chinese legend of a true heroine because she demonstrated the willingness to make the necessary sacrifices for family and homeland in the most noble tradition that fully incorporated revered ethical Confucian values that were the most historically esteemed by the Chinese people as a way-of-life in terms of ethics and morality.

All in all, the enduring legacy of Mulan has provided a powerful example that has inspired timeless lessons about the necessity of performing one's duty to God, homeland, and family, while emphasizing the equality of women and the importance of self-determination to rise higher in life and even in one of the most restrictive of all patriarchal societies.

Indeed, providing enduring lessons about how a powerless person held in low esteem in the male-dominated society can accomplish far beyond all expectations by relying upon her own intelligence, resourcefulness, and ingenuity, the beloved story of Mulan has especially emphasized the importance of loyalty to family and country in the most noble Chinese ethical and moral traditions that conformed to the most esteemed Confucian values upon which ancient Chinese society was based.

Therefore, the Mulan legend has been so warmly embraced by the Chinese people for centuries because of the extraordinary extent of her sense of duty and loyalty that far superseded in importance the fact that she had transgressed across gender boundaries to defy tradition, which had almost always resulted in societal disapproval.

Mulan also demonstrated that women could serve as wise and gifted leaders when in charge of large numbers of male fighting men in the warrior queen tradition, when she led her troops to victory against the so-called northern "barbarians," who threatened her people and homeland. In the process, she gained the immense favor of the Khan and his imperial court because of her heroics and skillful leadership that stood out from those of the men in the ranks.

The demonstration of the high level of Mulan's leadership qualities both on and off the battlefield during the stern challenges of wartime revealed a degree of wisdom, commitment to duty, and self-sacrifice that had been lacking in some male Chinese leaders, including those of high-rank, at this time. As so often the case, many male leaders, especially the most successful ones, often became corrupt and drunk with power in time when a series of victories bolstered their egos and arrogance. In contrast to some of these males in leadership positions, the self-sacrificing Mulan offered an inspiring example of a pristine level of purity in thought and deed that has long made this young woman the idol of her people, then and today.

In this sense during an age of the Chinese strongmen who ruled their people in an autocratic manner, Mulan's selfless example and leadership qualities provided an alternative case of a far more enlightened kind of thinking and leader, who put the Kahn and her people before her own welfare and life. Based on the timeless lessons of history and human nature, an old Chinese proverb has long emphasized how "the great man is a public misfortune," because of the corruptive influences of success and power, especially in wartime.

Of course, this ancient Chinese proverb that has been timeless was comparable to the western axiom that "absolute power corrupts absolutely," because, of course, human nature and its easy corruptibility have been one the same in either the East or West and regardless of the time period.

This ancient Chinese axiom has also verified truisms of the fate of many successful military leaders in the western experience that still apply to modern leaders today as much as in ancient times, because human nature has not changed over the centuries.

Significantly, the inspiring example of Mulan was the antithesis of the saying—based on centuries of experiences with Chinese warlords and strongmen—that "the great man is a public misfortune." In one historian's words of wisdom, this "sentiment aptly expresses the experience and wisdom of a peace-loving race. Were the victims of great men's glory to speak, not only in China but also almost anywhere, they would echo this homely judgment with signs and tears and curses."

By comparison, the refreshing example of a selfless and heroic Mulan has provided the opposite lessons that formed a fundamental basis of Confucian thought in regard to ethics in conducting one's life in a proper manner, as fully appreciated by the Chinese people for centuries: the supreme importance of loyalty to country and family, faithful service to a just ruler, purity of soul, and answering the call to duty in a righteous war. Of course, these noble qualities are still important lessons for people of all ages and races because they are still applicable when it comes character, duty, and sacrifice to this day.

Forgotten Non-Han Chinese Roots

The story of Mulan had been long considered an old Chinese fairy tale by many historians and scholars, especially in the West, but such is not the case. For the most part, this historic resistance to the core concepts of the Mulan legend has been a traditional male backlash because of what she achieved on her own—basically proving an equality to men by rising so high in the eyes of military men, including the Kahn and his imperial court, which was considered impossible for a woman—, which has been generally viewed as threatening to male egos, the fundamental beliefs of patriarchy, and the most basic concepts of male superiority.

First and foremost, these critics and disbelievers of the Mulan legend have long adhered to the traditional concept that military service was exclusively a male preserve and that a woman could not have possibly achieved what she accomplished by way of her own intelligence, skill, and savvy in the art of warfighting and inspired leadership.

However, recent modern science and archeology has demonstrated that warrior women were not myths as long assumed by the so-called experts, who have been almost exclusively male. Even more, recent scientific research has revealed that warrior women were far more common than has been generally assumed by generations of male historians and scholars, who might well be described as women warrior deniers, because of the vehemence and persistence their negative views about the possibility of female fighters.

Indeed, a good deal more evidence about the truth of large numbers of women warriors, including those who were leaders of their people, have been unearthed from recent archeology digs and investigations into ancient burial places, especially those of the ancient Scythian culture. Throughout the past, these burial mounds in the area around the Black Sea were all thought to have been exclusively the domain of male warriors, which we now know was certainly not the case.

The Scythians were a nomadic culture—like that of the people of Mulan's own Northern Wei Dynasty but much less so—whose members, male and female, rode across the steppes of Southwest Asia. However, the range of the Scythian people extended from the area around the Black Sea all the way east to Mongolia and nearly to the northwestern and western border of China. Thousands of miles of steppe connected Europe to Asia to dominate the heart of the Eurasian continent.

New DNA testing has recently revealed that many of these warrior skeletons, who were buried in wooden chamber tombs in earthen burial mounds—kurgans—with their cherished spears, lances, and swords, were indeed female warriors. In fact, around one-third of the skeletal remains that have been recently found in these mounds consisted of Scythian females: an extraordinary high percentage that revealed that women warriors were an accepted part of ancient Scythian society and culture, including the fact that there certainly existed a certain equality between male and female fighters not only in wartime but also in peacetime.

Just like male warriors, these female fighters, including respected leaders who rose high in Scythian warrior society, were found fully dressed for battle, including with their beloved war horses that had been buried with them. Significantly, such burial mounds revealed that these warrior women of the kurgans located on the steppes in the lower Don and Volga Rivers held high rank in their nomadic society, after having earned respect and prestige in the art of warfighting.

How could this rather remarkable development of such a large percentage of female warriors have been the case, especially when most male-written history has long denied their very existence? Even more, what conditions allowed for the rise of female warriors in Scythian society in the first place and more so than in other societies, especially in the West?

First and foremost, the combined factors of an unique geography and distinctive nomadic culture on the steppes around the Black Sea certainly played a leading role in this unique development of large numbers of warrior women on the world stage that was not seen so extensively a common phenomenon in other cultures and in other lands around the world, including in ancient China.

This unique situation that was a Scythian nomadic way-of-life on the vast expanse of the steppes amid an extremely harsh environment fostered greater equality for women, because everyone of this continuously moving society was needed to work closely together to maintain the tribal group in every way for the sake of simple survival on the open steppes. Basically, the Scythians followed their herds of domesticated animals across wide stretches of open country, while adjusting to the changes of seasons and the amount of grasses that was available for their domesticated animals on the steppes.

These hardy nomadic people survived by their resourcefulness in wisely utilizing the relatively few resources that were available and relying on expertise in the raising and herding of goats, sheep, yaks and horses. This kind of nomadic life in an extremely harsh environment often called for moving the entire village, while taking care of the vast herds for daily subsistence and driving them to greener pastures or into sheltering ravines, depending on the season.

The vulnerability of this nomadic society, which consisted of relatively small numbers of people constantly on the move in a hostile environment, placed a top priority on the art of warfighting and combat prowess. These stern requirements were necessary to defend a weak people of relatively small numbers against more powerful invaders, who could strike at any time on the wide expanse of the open steppe: a dangerous situation that called for a wider participation of warriors in regard to ages (both younger and older) and gender, both male and female, because of pressing wartime requirements and escalating threats.

Enjoying a rare equality to men like in everyday life in a harsh land of the open steppes, where trees were only found along ravines or rivers and creeks, for simple survival, Scythian women fought beside male warriors to defend their families, driving off invaders when it was a matter of life or death. When everyone was needed to fight beside each other for everyone's mutual survival because of the relatively small size of the nomadic band on the steppes, women early learned to ride horses, shot arrows with deadly accuracy, and slash with swords out of necessity for survival in a harsh world.

Because most steppe skirmishes and battles were fought on the open grasslands, men and women of Scythian society needed to be expert riders and archers, who could fire arrows from their bows across long distances with accuracy and while moving on horseback like their opponents.

The Amazons

In this way by utilizing as many people as possible as warriors, the tribal group survived because the women took a proactive role and fought in the ranks with the men as equals, while serving with pride and skill in protecting their people from the fierce raiders of the steppes. Most important from this situation, the rise of the Amazons of ancient Greek legends developed from the urgent need to survive on the steppes, while providing evidence of the development of a remarkable egalitarian society that existed between males and females, which flourished on the seemingly endless steppes of the Ukraine and Russia: a rare case of equality for women having been born out of the dangers of the wartime experience and times of crisis, when the life of the tribe was at stake.

According to ancient legend and then later verified by modern archeology, these Scythian warrior women were indeed the legendary Amazons, who had evolved into leading fighters and the defenders of their nomadic people, especially after most their men had been killed in battle: the natural evolution that led to the rise of legendary female fighters, who ensured their people's survival because of the establishment of the first known society dominated by females.

The native steppe homeland of the Scythians extended north far from the northern shore of the Black Sea into the wide expanse of open steppes of today's southern Ukraine and continued farther east across the open grasslands of Russia—historical facts and realities supported by the recent finds, especially in regard to warrior women, that have been discovered during extensive archeological searches into the burial mounds that have revealed a good many female warriors.

In a process that was all but inevitable because the survival of their society and families were at stake, the Scythians, or Amazons, were first recorded by the writings of ancient Greek historians and geographers. They informed their curious readers of the city-states about the female "barbarians" of an alien culture that thrived on the sprawling plains, which seemed to stretch forever. Unlike in other lands to such a dramatic extent, a most unique warrior women society had been created on the open steppes by way of a natural evolution out of urgent necessity and pressing requirements, because on the stern realities of their unforgiving environment.

To defend themselves and their families, especially children, and to reap an eagerly-revenge for the deaths of fathers, brothers, and husbands who had been killed by the steppe raiders, the Scythian women had first taken up arms in emergency situations. However, the concept of women warriors of the steppes was eventually incorporated on a permanent basis to provide the foundation of a matriarchal society led and dominated by females, after the loss of additional male lives—the legendary Amazons whose wartime exploits and martial skills shocked the ancient Greeks of a strict patriarchal society.

As noted, these warrior women of the steppes of today's Ukraine and Russia possessed able good reason to create a female warrior society that was dominated by a distinctive warrior ethos. After all, the capture of women by nomadic raiders, who were males of different ethnic groups in wars that were directed at the securing the precious meager resources of the steppes, resulted not only in slavery for captured women, but also longtime sexual abuse—the rest of their lives since this was a permanent slavery—as the concubines of the victors.

Therefore, these women fought fiercely, as emphasized by the ancient Greeks in their descriptive writings, when dressed like male warriors and fighting with the same determination. Indeed, fueling a superior motivation in desperate do-or-die situations, they fought like men to avoid such a cruel fate for themselves and their daughters, sisters and mothers, if overwhelmed by the opposition. In the traditional manner of war in ancient times and according to custom, all the males were killed by the raiders, while the women were taken into slavery, when a tribe was overwhelmed on the steppes.

All in all for a host of reasons, the Amazons evolved into legendary warriors of a distinctly matriarchal society of the sprawling steppes out of necessity in a wartime environment, because of the requirements of simple survival in a harsh world that was utterly Darwinian, or survival of the fittest: a situation that was not the case in Mulan's nomadic society of the Northern Wei Dynasty, which had been less under threat than in the case of the Scythians that led to the rise of the Amazons.

The Trojan War

Most important, these warrior women known as the Amazons (ancient Scythian females of the steppes) left a legacy of not only gaining personal independence but also earning a distinctive measure of equality with men that was rare, if not entirely unheard of, in the cultures and societies of the ancient Greek city-states, where women were kept in the lowest of positions in society.

This sad reality for ancient Greek females included daily life in the enlightened city-state of Athens, where equality and democracy were born, but not for women who continued to hold their lowly places in ancient Greek society. However, partly because of these reasons, the legacies of these Amazon fighters became part of ancient Greek culture in which they were correctly celebrated as exceptionally bold warriors, who the Greeks respected in their writings for their combat prowess and fierceness.

In western civilization's oldest heroic poem, just like the original source of Mulan's story stemmed from an ancient Chinese folk poem "The Ballad of Mulan," which was Homer's *Iliad*, the Amazons had played a key role during the final showdown between the invading Greeks and the Trojans on the battleground located just outside Troy's high walls near the end of the war. However, these women warriors have been the generally forgotten and most overlooked players in the final struggle for possession of the great city of Troy.

After Achilles had killed Hector during the most famous duel of the war and then dragged his bloody body three times around the city's walls behind his chariot, the Amazons, under Queen Penthesilea, arrived to bolster their Trojan allies in a timely manner. Indeed, at this time, Trojan spirits had fallen to new lows because of the tragic loss of the city's champion and finest warrior. Indeed, Prince Hector, who was the killer of seemingly countless Greek warriors, had been the leading fighter for the Trojans just like Achilles was the leading fighter among the Greeks.

Although small in number, the queen and her Amazon warriors, who wore bronze armor like the other antagonists and hid their long hair under their helmets like Mulan in another conflict that was destined to take place half way around the world, led the Trojan counterattack across the open plain that extended to the seashore, where the Greek ships were aligned next to each other.

After hard fighting that left the bodies of warriors strewn across the Trojan plain, the Amazons nearly reversed the war's course by their fierce fighting, while leading the rejuvenated Trojans in person. Interestingly, the Trojan male warriors had no hesitation about the fact that female fighters, headed by the queen herself, were leading their desperate charge, because of their well-deserved reputations as elite fighters in the Age of Bronze and the so-called Heroic Age.

Most important and as mentioned, the attack spearheaded by the Amazons lifted Trojan morale not long after Hector's death, and King Priam, who prayed to his Gods to save the city and still grieved as the father of the slain Hector although he had many sons, proudly proclaimed that the Amazon warriors were "a match for men in war." Even more, historian Herodotus described the hard-fighting Amazons as "killers of men," including Greek warriors, which was proven to be true on the Trojan Plain.

The Amazon's bravery and combat prowess that they demonstrated in full during their sweeping counterattack in leading the Trojans across the dusty plain even inspired large numbers of Trojan women, who were watching from the top of the city's high walls. They became so animated that the Trojan women set aside their traditional domestic duties, including the art of weaving (ironically, one of the same domestic skills of Mulan before she went to war, according to "The Ballad of Mulan), and then seized weapons to assist their men and fighting beside the Amazons, whose attack was succeeding against the fiercely resisting Greeks.

In fact, Troy's emboldened women were just about to depart through the city's gates to join the fight on the open plain that led to the sea, when they were deterred at the last minute by the priestess of Apollo. She sagely warned the armed women how the Amazons were experienced fighters, as good, if not better, than the men, unlike the thoroughly domesticated women of Troy. This wisdom brought the Trojan women to their senses and they laid down their weapons, allowing their men and the Amazons to do the fighting on the open plain now covered in bodies.

With the Amazons leading the way in the steamrolling counterattack, the Trojans pushed the Greeks all the way back to their flotilla of sailing ships that were lined up along the shore next to each other like a row of dominos. However, in the end, the Greeks rallied when Achilles organized the Greeks and then led the charge that met the Amazon and Trojan counterattack head-on beyond the row of sailing ships—the only way for the invaders to get back to Greece—that were under serious threat.

The reenergized Greeks, thanks to Achilles leading the way with sword and spear in hand, eliminated the Amazon warriors, who held the most advanced position before the Trojan's surging ranks, in a flurry of bloody hand-to-hand combat. Then, after a close-range contest, Achilles took the life of the Amazon queen, who gave the Greek champion more than a challenge, that ensured the repulse of the Trojan counterattack.

The defeated Trojans then fled back toward their city, carrying their wounded fighters with them, after a bloody showdown in which most of the Amazons had been killed. They had bravely died with their queen, battling courageously to the bitter end.

Thereafter, as Homer related, Troy was doomed and shortly fell to the Greeks by the famous treachery of the ruse of the Trojan Horse that contained some of the finest Greek warriors, such as Odysseus, after the repulse of the Amazon-led counterattack that had made significant gains, before having been hurled back toward the city's gates. In the usual formula of Bronze Age victors, the Greeks killed all the males and took the women as slaves, after they had flooded into Troy once the city's gates had been opened by Odysseus and his men.

As usual to verify the alleged cultural and intellectual superiority over the so-called "barbarian" societies, including the Amazons who hailed from the vast remoteness of the Eurasian steppes, the ancient Greek writers always had their most revered heroes, especially Achilles, prevailing over their less civilized enemies to provide a moral lesson to Greek audiences.

Indeed, what the ancient Greek writers emphasized was the lesson of what disastrous developments—the moral of the story—would result if the cherished values of their patriarchal society were turned outside down in a world in which the unthinkable occurred when females ruled a society of warrior women, who possessed the audacity to have boldly asserted themselves over men: the ultimate horror of horrors to the males of the ancient Greek world, which was not unlike in the prevalent thinking of males in many modern societies even to this day.

This situation was a natural, if not inevitable, development in the history of patriarchal societies from ancient times to the modern world in which the importance of women's roles have been entirely overlooked or dismissed by males for centuries, especially by generations of male historians.

Scholars and historians have long believed that the Amazons were nothing more than fantasy figures that stemmed from the vivid imaginations of ancient Greeks— a titillating subject for sexually-curious males—and mere imaginary myths like mighty Zeus and other mythological Greek Gods, who capriciously dictated the fates of men for their own amusement. However, in truth and as mentioned, what has long been considered as myths and legends about the Amazons since the days of the ancient Greeks, warrior women from the steppes of Central Asia and Southwest Asia were in fact true, as an ever-increasing amount of new scientific evidence has proven to have been the case by the second decade of the twenty-first century.

As noted, this fundamental truth about large numbers of women warriors, including when they served as the leaders of male fighters, has been verified by recent archeological studies of ancient Scythian burial mounds, where the remains of a good many warrior women were found to be buried: much like the relatively recent scientific and archeological verification of the ancient city of Troy located on the north African coast that has also given much more tangible proof and verification that the Trojan War was not a myth as assumed by scholars and historians, including ancient history experts, for centuries.

Consequently, in the end, the ancient Greek, including Homer and the father of all historians Herodotus, were correct in their ancient stories that told about the courage and lethality of the Amazons, who fought as male warriors and often triumphed over Greek male warriors.

Indeed, despite their limited knowledge about world geography and history, the ancient Greeks believed that these female warriors hailed from ancient nomadic societies in and around the Black Sea. As mentioned, this ancient view of Greek historians and scholars was in fact right on target because this region was part of the cherished homeland of the ancient Scythians, where these warrior women had made ever-lasting names for themselves.

To the ancient Greeks and as revealed in their mythological tales of Gods and heroes, these warrior women, or Amazons, were entirely deserving of respect, if not awe, because of their courageous actions and combat prowess when they proved themselves to be "equals of men," which was fully demonstrated on the battlefield.

Indeed, the ancient Greeks had long praised the valor of these Scythian warrior women, who were known for their skill with weapons and horse riding, which included firing arrows from horseback while on the move at a brisk pace. Like no other women of the ancient world, these female fighters won the undying admiration of the ancient Greeks also because the Greeks possessed an infantry-oriented military (they relied on the much-revered helots who were armored infantrymen and who fought in the famous Greek phalanx that had proved so devastating to the invading Persians under King Xerxes in 480 B.C.) and not cavalry.

Ancient Greek stories told of some of their greatest heroes, including Heracles and Achilles, having battled these highly-skilled Amazon warriors, who were exceptionally skilled in the combat capabilities, including hand-to-hand fighting. Interestingly, ancient Greek tales, including the outlandish story that Amazons physically removed one of their breasts to perfect their archery skills to enhance their drawing back of the bow, about the hard-fighting Amazon warriors fascinated ancient Greek audiences, just like modern audiences are fascinated by the heroic story of Mulan to this day.

Most often, the ancient Greek heroes, especially Achilles who killed the Amazon queen on the Trojan Plain during the final phase of the Trojan War, were portrayed in the role of overcoming these Amazon warriors during hand-to-hand combat in a simple morality tale. These dramatic battle scenes between Amazons and Greek warriors from the days of the heroic past were depicted on a good many ancient Greek art objects, including fine pottery, including as exquisite vases.

Such revered art objects were crafted by generations of talented Greek artists, who played their part in keeping alive the memory and legacy of the fierce-fighting Amazons. Therefore, even the common people of ancient Greece possessed knowledge about the Amazons from what they had seen on art objects, including those items that people used on a daily basis.

Ironically, while the courage and equality displayed by the Scythian warrior women, including when fighting on horseback that demonstrated their equestrian and archery skills gained in steppe warfare, were celebrated by the ancient Greeks, they failed to hold their own women in such high esteem. Indeed, at the same time, the ancient Greeks ensured that their women, especially wives, remained little more than lowly domestics without equality that was enjoyed and celebrated by the Amazons: one of the strange contradictions of ancient Greek society in which freedom and equality were the most cherished of values. Clearly, the subject of women warriors has provided a timeless fascination to millions of people from ancient times and to this day.

In truth, the stories of ancient female warriors have persisted in many lands around the world to a degree, but they have not generally recognized or appreciated by generations of male scholars and historians. Instead, for centuries, the perspective of most male historians and scholars have been considerably narrowed by their more male-oriented and nationalist focus rather than an international and female-oriented focus that was needed to ascertain broad universal patterns of human behavior, especially in regard to warrior women.

Throughout the course of history and in many lands, including in ancient China, women have often risen high above their male peers to become dynamic leaders and the commanders of armies that marched to victory against foreign invaders during times of national crisis.

Queen Boadicea, who has continued to be revered today in England by generations of Britons like Mulan has been the favorite heroine of the Chinese people, was one such warrior queen, who boldly rose to the fore. With great bravery, she led her oppressive Celtic people against the hated ancient Romans, who had invaded the Albion island. Like Mulan to the Chinese people, so Boadicea has remained a cultural icon to this day in England, where she is honored and celebrated.

Ancient Roman writers, like Tacitus, wrote about the courage and leadership skill of Boadicea in leading the 60 and 61 A.D. revolt of her Celtic tribe against the highly-touted Roman legions. Like Mulan's legend has been long embraced by the Chinese people, so Boadicea has long captured the imagination of the English people, who had dedicated statues to her.

However, Boadicea was hardly the first warrior queen, who led mostly males in battle against foreign invaders. In leading her people and defending her homeland of Britain, Queen Boadicea had followed in the footsteps of another warrior queen, Pharaoh Hatshepsut of Egypt. During the fifteenth century B.C., Hatsheput led a campaign of thousands of warriors against Nubia, which lay farther up the Nile River to the south.

Generations of ancient warrior women fought against the enemies of their people from the sun-baked deserts to snow-bound lands. In addition and like on the wide steppes of the Ukraine, the archeology of ancient graves in Sweden have proved the existence of Viking women warriors. These new finds have revealed that these women also fought beside the men as full-fledged warriors against their enemies. Buried with weapons and warhorses like the Scythian women warriors around the Black Sea, an increasingly number of skeletons in the north country of Sweden have revealed, thanks to DNA testing, that these were prestigious warrior women, including leaders who made key decisions, including tactical plans during wartime.

Like the female fighters of the Scythians, the Sweden excavations of ancient burial sites have been still another case of what has been long considered nothing more than legend and myths—warrior women of the north—were in fact true. In this sense and like in ancient Chinese and Greek history, ancient Viking lore about the stirring roles of warrior women has proved to be true because of the recent finds of modern archeology and science to verify what had been long considered romantic myths created by imaginative writers and historians of the ancient past.

As noted and most significantly, the phenomenon of women warriors has been far more widespread than originally thought. Consequently, given a host of factors, both old and new, the distinct possibly does exist that Mulan was not a purely Chinese story as long thought, because of the widespread universality of warrior women that existed in Mongolia north of China.

It is not known but Mulan's story possibly might well have originally developed from the experience of the Chinese of the north in having first learned—by fighting against them—about the Scythian female warrior raiders of the steppes, which extended into Mongolia, who had long raided western and northern China in ancient times. However, this theory is mere speculation and cannot be verified.

Indeed, created on the northern frontier where the nomadic raiders from Mongolia had long struck with a vengeance and from a conflict in which "The Ballad of Mulan" had emerged, China possessed its most popular female warrior tradition in Mulan that was very likely partly based on the northern Chinese people of the Northern Wei Dynasty having faced hard-fighting Scythian females.

As noted and in a tradition not seen in northern China among the non-Han ethnic group of which Mulan was a member, these hard-riding women of the steppes had originally evolved from having initially fought beside males to protect themselves and their families to become aggressive raiders in their own right—the Amazons—on the open steppes, including the targeting of towns on the Chinese frontier.

But, by far, the greatest amount of evidence has revealed that Mulan was an authentic Chinese heroine, but an ethnic one or non-Han, and that ancient Chinese folk history was in fact true, partly because a distinguished warrior women tradition of China had existed long before Mulan. For the most part, the fundamental truths of Mulan's legacy can be seen in the fact that her legend has fit neatly into the overall pattern of dynamic ancient Chinese women, who fought as men over the course of centuries.

However, Mulan has stood out as the most notable example of an ancient Chinese woman who had made the bold decision to serve her family and people in the disguise of a male warrior in wartime, and whose remarkable story has evolved into a folk tale that has endured to this day with renewed vigor because of the modern media. Indeed, Mulan has only stood out from a long cast of Chinese women warriors and leaders because her tale has been more warmly embraced by the Chinese people than any other in history.

In this sense, Mulan had long been the chosen one and favorite of the Chinese people before she became an international icon.

In truth and in the context of an overall historical perspective, consequently, the story of Mulan actually revealed nothing unusual or odd in the course of Chinese history because of the distinguished tradition of ancient Chinese women warriors that has existed over such a long period of time throughout the course of ancient Chinese history.

Indeed, China, like other Asian nations, has warmly embraced the concept of warrior women for centuries and long before America's discovery and the overall acknowledgement of the West's own warrior women heritage and without question or debate, because these female fighters have been for so long deeply ingrained in Chinese culture on multiple levels.

As noted, a lengthy list of ancient Chinese heroines existed both before and after Mulan and her time period, and the Chinese people early accepted the truths about Mulan's story because of the fundamental and undeniable realities of other equally dynamic ancient Chinese warrior women, who have earned distinction in the annals of ancient Chinese history. Consequently, Mulan early became a national heroine among the Chinese people and nothing has changed to this day in this regard.

What cannot be debated was the fact that Mulan was able to gain a new sense of identity, independence, and autonomy as a woman warrior and dynamic leader unlike any previous endeavor in her life, when she performed her martial feats on the battlefield, while wearing her father's suit of armor that she had admired as a young girl in a more innocent time: a true liberating experience second to none during the course of Mulan's eventful life.

During numerous campaigns against the northern enemies of her people over a period of years, she gained a great deal of pride in fighting for her family, country, and people, while excelling in a wartime environment disguised as a male warrior, who managed to faithfully keep her secret over an extended period of time. Even more, Mulan also gained supreme satisfaction in doing her duty to the best of her ability and upholding the honor of her family, especially her aged father who had been too old and infirm to go to war. In this sense, Mulan was like a surrogate son, fighting for the honor of her father because he could not.

What has been generally overlooked was the fact that Mulan, after she had been empowered by her own initiative and actions after her family had attempted to dissuade her, rejoiced in having outsmarted and outwitted so many males, who had long held women in lowly places in a strict patriarchal society. All the while, she successfully defended her homeland by the success in her disguise and actions for years—estimated to have been around a decade of continuous warfare—, which were the epitome of the time-honored definitions of masculinity and the core values of a patriarchal society, although she retained her femininity in a careful disguise which she kept carefully hidden from her male comrades from beginning to end.

It is not known with any degree of certainty but Mulan must have privately rejoiced when alone and off the battlefield in the knowledge of having gotten away with her clever disguise—traditional warrior's garb, including her father's suit armor—for years in order for her to perform her duty to her people, family, and the Kahn, while neatly circumventing all of the traditional anti-woman prejudices and severe constraints that had been long directed against her gender for no other reason than her sex.

Of course, what was most remarkable about the story of young Chinese woman from the Northern Wei Dynasty was how she has become a modern phenomenon, evolving into a cultural icon not only in America, but also around the world by the early twenty-first century.

In the most amazing of transformations, an ancient Chinese folk tale—originally in the form of an extremely short and non-specific ancient poem by an unknown author—about a remarkable young woman, who lived centuries ago has become an universal and iconic story that has been warmly embraced today by millions of people around the world like no other female figure in history.

An Old Enemy

Indeed, the fact that Mulan has gained iconic status to become an international legend and success story today has been nothing less than a remarkable development on a global level. After all, parts of United States society, especially right-wing conservative and including high-ranking members of the American military establishment, have long considered China as the number one threat to American national security.

This development has especially been the case in the twenty-first century after China has significantly increased in power, both economically and militarily, to challenge America's dominant position in the world as a military and economic rival.

Even more, it was not that long ago in America that China was widely viewed as the ultimate enemy in terms of a world threat and representative of evil on the world stage like in today's extreme conservative and ultra-nationalist circles in the United States, when the West confronted the threat of the rising tide of Communism in the post-Second World War period.

During the Cold War and like its Soviet Union ally, China posed a threat to America, especially by the aggressive spread of Communism around the world. Because China and the Soviet Union were the foremost Communist powers in the post-Second World War world, the United States was ideologically pitted against their expansionism to spread the Communist doctrine to lands across the Third World.

Of course, this fear of the spread of Communism was one of the fundamental reasons for America's ill-fated involvement during the long war in Vietnam in Southeast Asia beginning in the 1960s and then well into the 1970s. During the decade and a half of conflict and like the Soviet Union, China openly supported North Vietnam as a faithful ally, supplying America's enemy with arms and munitions.

However, in truth, anti-Chinese sentiment in the United States had reached an all-time high more than a generation before in the previous decade during the Korean War of 1950 to 1953. To this day, animosity toward China is alive and well in some circles in the United States in part because knowledge of the Chinese people and their rich ancient history among generations of Americans have been historically extremely low or practically non-existent.

However, this dark legacy has not hampered the popularity of the story of Mulan across the breath of America, thanks largely to Disney and new generations of Americans, who have possessed relatively little knowledge of their own history and the historical past in general (the so-called "dumbing down" of America has been occurring for generations in the United States school system, especially in regard to properly teaching the nation's history) and much less than most other countries around the world.

However, for a host of reasons, the story of Mulan has been closely embraced by Americans today in a culturally significant development that would not have been possible in the United States during most of the twentieth century. Mulan has become not only fully acceptable and believable to the American people today, but also the legend has been warmly embraced by them because the nation itself has thoroughly changed culturally and demographically, especially by becoming a more inclusive country and more than any time during the past by the twenty-first century.

Therefore, Disney's release of its first Mulan film in 1998 was timely because so many of the old anti-China views and anti-China prejudices had already began to significantly diminish among Americans by the last years of the twentieth century. This development that has represented a significant cultural shift can be partly explained by the dying out of the Korean War generation— the last generation of Americans who fought against Chinese troops in the early 1950s.

The bitter warfare between United States troops and the forces of China erupted when large numbers of Chinese troops were unleashed in October 1950 because American and NATO [North Atlantic Treaty Organization] forces had approached the Yalu River, or China's southern border, after pushing South Korean forces north and liberating the south. At that time, American servicemen had thwarted the effort to spread North Korean Communism (Chinese Communism) from taking control of South Korea, and then had pushed far north.

Today over half a century since the end of the Korean War, more than 20 million Chinese-Americans live in the United States and significantly contribute to the nation's cultural richness and heritage on a wide variety of levels. Of course, the answer to the central question of how an ancient Chinese folk heroine from so many centuries ago became so popular in America and around the world by the twenty-first century is a relatively simple one.

First and foremost, the story of Mulan today is big business in the United States, generating billions of dollars in the world market, thanks large to the expert commercialism and global reach of the Disney Company. Quite simply and to this day, Disney has thoroughly exploited this fascinating subject like no other in the last more than two decades.

And the immense popularity of this young ancient Chinese woman, who had evolved from a real person into one of mythical status in a process that began even in ancient times, has continued to rise higher to this day and to entirely unprecedented levels. For nearly two decades, Disney has exploited a vast international market with the Mulan story to reap a great amount of profits that have served as a primary source of a massive amount of income flowing into the company coffers. And, significantly, this sophisticated process of commercializing and brand marketing in the telling of Mulan's story has been continued unabated today by the marketers at Disney.

During the first week of September 2020, Disney finally released its full-lengthy feature movie *Mulan*. This final release date had been delayed because of the outbreak and spread of the coronavirus epidemic around the world, including in China which was the source of the virus, in early 2020. Again, the Mulan character has been so lucrative throughout the past that the Disney Company has been able to repeat its astounding success of capitalizing on the Mulan legend for decades and to this day: first, the immensely-successful and profitable 1998 animated film *Mulan* that set the stage for future efforts by Disney.

This was Disney's first Mulan effort in the company's long history that had never previously featured a Chinese main character, which has been a revolutionary development. One of the company's most profitable efforts of all time, this first Disney film in the late 1990s was so successful that *Mulan II* was released in 2005 to additionally capitalize on this intriguing subject that has long captivated people around the world.

Most important, Disney has played the largest role in bringing a new vision to the world by telling the Mulan story in three movies in what has resulted in a truly revolutionary development around the globe: changing the world view about women, especially Chinese females, by helping to overturn longtime negative stereotypes by revealing what woman can achieve on their own and just like males as personified by Mulan.

From the beginning, Disney films about Mulan have been extremely lucrative across the breath of a vast international and global market like no other subject for the company during an extremely profitable period of more than a generation: an unmatched economic boon based on Disney's longtime commercial tactic and winning formula of turning some of the world's most popular characters of folk tales and fairy tales into major film creations that had proved immensely successful and profitable decade after decade.

In its most recent effort and as mentioned, Disney's release of the long-awaited *Mulan* was finally been rescheduled for Friday September 4, 2020. At long last, the film appeared in many theaters to an eager public around the world. As could be expected with profits in mind, this eagerly-anticipated $200,000 film was basically a remake of the animated 1998 film that proved so successful for the Disney Company.

The September 4, 2020 release date was also significant because it continued to reveal a profound evolution of more positive and enlightened thought in America about both women and China, which coincided with western women, especially in the United States, continuing to gain more equality in society in general during the twenty-first century.

Indeed and most revealing, only relatively recently has the story of warrior women become generally accepted by the general public in the United States—historically, a strict patriarchal society in which women have long struggled for their fundamental and basic rights, including the right to vote for women which was finally won by them in 1919—, like in the Civil War community of male historians who have discounted the concept of women warriors, because of the extent of the longtime societal and cultural bias against women that have ensured their lowly status as second class citizens: a most unfortunate situation, which has existed long since the nation's birth and despite its idealized promise of equality for all, which was a deferred promise for many generations of American women like for African Americans.

Even more, the United States had long been excessively xenophobic toward Eastern cultures, especially that of China, and its seemingly mysterious ways and Asian people in general. Like African Americans, so Asian people in America were long experienced hostility and discrimination that had been incorporated into state and national laws that were race-based during the nineteenth century and well into the twentieth century. And, of course, of all individuals from China, Chinese-American women in American society have been the most marginalized and ignored much like African American women throughout the course of American history.

Of course, the most notable example of discrimination against Asians was witnessed at the beginning of America's entry into the Second World War. The United States' sudden entry into the world conflict resulted when the Japanese air and naval forces attacked America's Pearl Harbor naval and army base on Hawaii on the fateful morning of December 7, 1941.

When war hysteria and anti-Asian sentiment ran exceptionally high across America because of the shock of the disaster and high loss of American lives at Pearl Harbor, President Franklin D. Roosevelt ordered the placement of tens of thousands of Japanese-American citizens—full-fledged and productive members of American society—on the West Coast in internment camps in California, because of the badly-misplaced fear that they would side with their mother country in the war and commit acts of sabotage.

Of course, however, these Japanese-Americans, who were only attempting to make their American Dream come true on the west coast, were almost all faithful and loyal citizens to the adopted country and loved America just like non-Asian American citizens. Therefore, ironically, they were patriotic citizens, and a sizeable number of Japanese-Americans served with honor and distinction in the United States military during the Second World War, especially in the Pacific Theater.

For such reasons and in overall historical terms in regard to China, perhaps no outside culture and society in any land around the world has been less known in America and to the American people for a longer period of time. Indeed, even in the twenty-first century, it can be said that Americans in general know less about the Chinese people and their rich history over the centuries than any other foreign culture on earth. For instance, the vast majority of Americans today across the nation do not personally know any Chinese-American citizens, much less having them as friends of their families, especially in America's remote rural areas.

And, of course in overall historical terms in regard to immigrants, including migrating whites like the Irish people from the Emerald Isle for generations, from distant lands, the United States had long discriminated against the Chinese from the very beginning of their story in America that began in the nineteenth century.

Therefore, for such reasons, it has been all the more remarkable that the inspirational story of Mulan has been so enthusiastically embraced today by Americans of all ages, genders, and races—since the last years of the twentieth century thanks to Disney's successful global commercialism—by a nation that historically has been xenophobic to the extreme toward foreigners.

For a wide variety of reasons, the story of the Chinese in both Asia and America has been one of the most forgotten and overlooked subjects to the citizens of the United States to this day. In this sense and like their rich history, the Chinese have truly become the most ignored and forgotten people in America, especially in regard to their roles in the making of America, including in the settlement of the Old West.

By 1880 and thanks largely to the 1849 California Gold Rush, more than 300,000 Chinese migrated to America and lived in the United States, mostly in California. The Chinese played a key role in the making of not only California, but also America.

However, the unfortunate historical reality of obscurity has revealed the overall negative situation in regard to the contributions of the Chinese people—the forgotten people of America's story, including in the Old West's settlement—and their rich history: a situation that has made today's immense popularity of Mulan in the United States even more remarkable in overall terms.

Thanks to the modern media, especially the efforts of the Disney Company during more than last two decades, the story of Mulan has presented a most uplifting story about the empowerment of a young Chinese woman by way of her own bold and selfless efforts to inspire people around the world to this day. This inspirational influence has been especially the case for a good many young women, regardless of race, society, and culture, who have found an ideal role model in this young Chinese warrior woman, who fought with her heart for family and country: an endless and timeless lesson of the importance of the key values of self-sacrifice and love for values that were larger than herself.

Indeed, the fascinating story of Mulan has provided today's young women, regardless of culture and country, with an inspirational example of the supreme importance of seizing her own personal destiny to rise higher in life on one's own merits and abilities. Mulan's life has provided an inspirational example of a powerless person in a patriarchal society boldly accepting greater challenges and doing what males have long considered impossible for women to achieve in life.

To successfully cope with life's seemingly endless and often insurmountable challenges for young women in the twenty-first century in both the East and the West, what is especially needed for women in today's environment might well be described as the Mulan can-do spirit, which she demonstrated in full during her incredible story of female empowerment. Indeed, the enduring lessons of history and Mulan's life have presented a host of valuable life lessons to young women in the twenty-first century because they are truly timeless.

As mentioned, the fascinating story of Mulan has become so popular in the United States today partly because the nation has evolved for the better, changing culturally and demographically by the twenty-first century to enthusiastically embrace a young woman from ancient Chinese history like no other woman, including American females partly because of the lack of knowledge about America's own distinguished warrior women heritage, which is an incredibly rich one.

Because the United States has become a more inclusive nation toward minorities, including its Chinese-American citizens, in the twenty-first century, this ancient Chinese folk tale has gained a great amount of popularity in the American consciousness and memory—a level of embracement by the nation of a foreign figure, especially a woman, that would have not been possible during most of the twentieth century to such as degree as witnessed in the United States during the twenty-first century.

Therefore, despite the fact that China has evolved into a major world power and a primary rival to the United States by the late twentieth century and in the twenty-first century, the time has never been better, or so it seemed, than now for the release of a full-length movie about Mulan—the long-awaited Disney release date finally became a reality on Friday September 4, 2020—, because this young Chinese warrior of the Northern Wei Dynasty had become not only a national icon in America, but also a world icon in an unprecedented development.

However, in fact and to the surprise of the Disney Company's top executives, a number of recent political developments far beyond the United States' borders, especially human rights violations of ethnic minorities in northern China—the ancestral homeland of the Uighurs who are Chinese Muslims—by the Chinese Communist Government, made this release date one of the worst of all times for the Disney Company. However, Disney was unable to anticipate these developments and the rise of pro-human rights and pro-democracy protests against the repressive actions of the Chinese government around the world.

As mentioned, this current author has long focused on revealing the truth about the prevalence of warrior women in his multi-volume series of books that have told the remarkable true stories of courageous fighting females from a variety of lands, races, and cultures: Haitian Revolutionary women who performed heroically, including sacrificing their lives, during the struggle for freedom against Napoleon's Bonaparte's forces who were attempting to restore slavery; Harriet Tubman, a former Maryland slave who was a leading conductor of the Underground Railroad during the 1850s and engaged in active military roles in the Civil War, and female Buffalo Soldier Cathy Williams, a former slave who served for nearly two years in the United States Army disguised as a man in a Buffalo Soldier regiment in the Old West not long after the Civil War's conclusion.

Consequently, this current "new look" view of Mulan and the political controversy that has surrounded the early September 2002 release of Disney's *Mulan* has continued the current author's longtime tradition of promoting the fascinating true stories of distinguished warrior women around the world and giving these deserving feminist pioneers and trendsetters, regardless of their race or nation of origin, their rightful and proper due in the historical record. After all, they were all ahead of their time since today's militaries of the world, including of the United States, contain large numbers of female military personnel.

One of the best ways to fully understand Mulan, her inspirational influence, and the modern impact of her distinguished legacy has come from the revealing words and hopes of young Chinese women today. Therefore, this book has taken a close look at the dramatic impact of the legend of Mulan on women's lives today. The words of contemporary Chinese-Americans have been able to inform and enlighten us about the real Mulan and her true meaning and legacy in the lives of these young women during the twenty-first century.

After all, the patriarchal oppression and harsh discrimination experienced for centuries by Chinese women has continued to have a significant impact today as part of an oppressive patriarchal cultural legacy: hence, the importance of Mulan's enlightening story because it has played a role in overcoming this dark legacy by empowering young women today.

Of course, this historic male oppression of females in the patriarchal tradition of ancient China was a factor that partly caused Mulan to respond with a spirited defiance that led her to become a warrior woman and it has also explained her timeless popularity to this day, especially in having overcome the odds in an unjust system of female oppression long perpetuated by male-dominated societies around the world.

Consequently and as noted, this current book has included the insightful views and opinions of modern Chinese-American women in regard to their admiration and respect for warrior women, especially Mulan, and how the enduring legacy of Mulan's story has shaped their own destinies in positive and inspirational ways.

This current book, therefore, has taken a fresh look at Mulan and her inspirational legacy today and the modern controversary that has been generated by the 2020 Disney film to better understand how Mulan has become a symbol of female independence and freedom against the abuses of a discriminatory patriarchal world. Today around the world, countless numbers of girls and young women have continued to admire Mulan's success in her personal quest for freedom in the face of an ancient society's anti-female injustices and inequalities.

In her own unique way by disguising herself as a male warrior and serving for years in battling the enemies of her people of the Northern Wei Dynasty and in purely spiritual terms, Mulan rejoiced from having escaped from the restrictive bonds of womanhood to gain a distinctive measure of equality and personal freedom that was so rare in her day of excessive female oppression and domination. Mulan's desire for greater freedom, mobility, and autonomy helped to propel her and her unique warrior ways into the realm of legend and to iconic status around the world in the twenty-first century.

By winning unique distinction in the annals of Chinese history as a courageous female warrior who battled for honor, family, and God, Mulan secured the ultimate sense of freedom from the heavy weight and burden of traditional male oppression of females that was deeply-ingrained in Chinese society and culture for centuries, when her spirit soared to new heights while she courageously battled against the enemies of her northern China people for an extended period of time.

Even more, Mulan forcefully demonstrated an almost unimaginable and remarkable level of equality to men during the challenges of wartime by exhibiting a great deal of bravery, character, and commitment to family and her beloved homeland, when the trials of combat, especially hand-to-hand fighting, was the ultimate test of masculinity around the world and since time immemorial.

Chapter II

The Historical Mulan

First and foremost and as expected by her Confucian society, Mulan was a very good daughter who lived in an extremely strict patriarchal society of the nomadic Xianbei people in northern China.

However, in general and although minimal, she possessed a level of greater equality in her nomadic society rather than if she had been part of a non-nomadic society located farther from the frontier and deeper into China. These nomads, who were Mulan's people, were members of the Tuoba clan that was part of the Northern Wei Dynasty located in north China below the southern border of Mongolia and one based on traditional Confucian ethical values.

These cherished values of the Confucians were based on a rational set of ethics that defined how to conduct a decent and rewarding way-of-life, including reverence for ancestors. As part of the ages' old philosophy of Confucianism, the ancestors and family, therefore, were the most important priorities in Mulan's life when she came of age. Before she became a woman warrior and served with distinction for more than a decade, Mulan seemed destined for the most ordinary of lives that had been long automatically ordained for a domestic role as a future wife and mother as expected by her family and society, because of her gender and lowly status as a female.

As part of a non-Han (the Han were the majority of people in China in ancient times and like today) ethnic group and nomadic society in northern China, Mulan lived with her family and engaged in all of the traditional duties and roles of the good daughter of her class and station in Chinese society.

The earliest account of her life—"The Ballad of Mulan"—has portrayed Mulan engaged in the typically feminine domestic chore of weaving at the loom that was located by the front door of the family home. She was still a virgin without a boyfriend as a young woman, despite her attractiveness. According to "The Ballad of Mulan," she "did not have a man she was in love with [and] There was no boy who occupied her thoughts."

Clearly, before the rise of the "barbarian" threat to her people and homeland by invasions from the north in Mongolia, Mulan existed in what can be described as the most ordinary, if not boring, of lives like other female members of her non-Han ethnic group.

As mentioned, Mulan's ethnic group was almost certainly that of the Touba (also known as Toba) clan of the Xianbei people of northern nomads, who had established the Northern Wei Dynasty and ruled in the north from 386 to 534. However, this dynasty was threatened from the north when Mulan was in her formative years, and the extent of this threat was destined to change her life forever.

What was the extent and nature of the "barbarian threat" from the north that had descended upon the people of the Northern Wei Dynasty? From the steppes to the north in Mongolia, these distinctive nomadic non-Han invaders, including warrior women, were experts in horseback riding and the use of the bow and arrow. Some female fighters among these raiders from the north served beside male fighters in the tradition of the Scythian women warriors, or the so-called Amazons, especially after these legendary women had grown in numbers to dominate their nomadic society that became matriarchal in consequence.

In regard to Mulan's inspirational legacy that has continued to thrive to this day, what has been fully embraced by China and then the West has been primarily a non-Han Chinese tradition and ancient folk tale that was founded on the courage and combat prowess of northern nomadic women. What is now clear was the fact that Mulan was not the only woman warrior on her nomadic society and, of course, in other societies in ancient China, although she was the most famous.

The people of the Northern Wei Dynasty had fought for generations against northern invaders from Mongolia. Therefore, the distinct possibility existed that Mulan was but only a representative and symbolic example of the warrior women of her nomadic society in the north.

In her early years while growing up as a member of the Northern Wei Dynasty that was located just south of Mongolia and as mentioned, nothing at all seemed to have marked Mulan for any kind of distinction whatsoever. She seemed to be an ordinary young woman because that was indeed the case, except for having an early interest in her father's past army career, his armor and sword, and the martial arts.

From her days of early childhood, Mulan's future had been already long ordained for her by her family and society—a future life of a good wife and mother destined for nothing more than a quiet and peaceful domestic role like hundreds of thousands of women across the breath of China, because this was her primary duty to her family and society in the Confucian tradition.

From the beginning, consequently, a strong sense of duty defined the life of young Mulan in every way, and this duty-bound responsibility was part of the fiber of her being for as long as she could remember. Duty was a most highly-valued quality that was important to Mulan from an early age because it was a core foundation of her northern nomadic society society and culture because it was bound to the Confucian concept of honor and personal dignity.

Therefore, she faithfully performed her domestic duties because they were fully expected of her without question by the family and as required of a good daughter: ironically, a strong sense of duty that was destined to eventually convince her to boldly accept the challenge of going to war for the honor of her family and as a surrogate fighter for his disabled father. Most of all and as noted, Mulan was a good daughter and sibling, which made her family proud during the years before the menacing threat from Mongolia to the north suddenly once again reemerged to jeopardize the existence of her people and the Khan's lands.

However, from an early age, Mulan was different from the vast majority of young women, who were primarily focused on needlework and weaving and other traditional duties in the female domestic realm, of her clan in the Northern Wei Dynasty. But in fact, Mulan was a most extraordinary young woman, whose most redeeming qualities were still hidden and overshaded by the shroud of female domesticity that was part of everyday life. However, deep inside Mulan lay the heart of a true warrior that was disguised by a quiet life of peace, the dictates of tribal tradition, Confucianism, and everyday normality.

At first, this heart of the warrior of Mulan had been only slowly and gradually hinted at an early age and in a relatively subtle manner, ensuring that no one noticed but her father. As a tomboy without a boyfriend at this time and because of her closeness to her father who still revered his past military service like most former veterans of past wars when they had been young, she possessed an early interest in the martial arts, including how to ride a horse and use a bow and arrow with skill.

As could be expected because of the strength of their special bond that existed between father and daughter, this early interest in martial arts demonstrated by Mulan had been first encouraged by her father. After all, he was still extremely proud of what he had performed as a combat veteran of previous wars and as a younger man and his memories of his days of glory were still vivid.

In some ways, he seemed to view Mulan almost as a surrogate son despite her lack of traditional male qualities and characteristics. After all, Mulan's interest in her father's distinguished wartime past and his suit of armor and sword, which were prized possessions of the entire family, allowed him to relieve old battles to his wide-eyed daughter, when he had been at the peak of his strength and health in better days.

Because of his daughter's early interest in martial arts at a formative age, he early began to teach her how to defend herself. All in all, this was a wise decision because Mulan's family of the Northern Wei Dynasty lived near the Mongolian border, where nomadic raiders thrived and occasionally launched raids to the south.

For such reasons, he naturally felt a good deal of fatherly concern about his daughter's future welfare, when the raiders from the north might strike again to catch everyone by surprise, especially at nighttime. In consequence, Mulan's father understood how teaching his daughter about martial arts was the best way for Mulan to be able to protect herself against any male threats. And such threats included from kidnappers, bandits, and especially in wartime when the raiders from Mongolia desired nothing more than to capture young Northern Wei Dynasty women for lifetime concubines and slaves.

Mulan's father even taught her how to use his most prized possession—his cherished sword from his wartime days in the distant past, when he had battled with tenacity for the preservation of his people. Naturally very proud of his past wartime service in which he had distinguished himself and as noted, Mulan's father kept his full suit of armor as a prized possession in the house that Mulan called home, and she had admired it for as long that she could remember.

Unlike the full-body armor of medieval Europe that consisted of a single piece of metal to eliminate a knight's flexibility when mobility and dexterity were most of all needed in close combat situations with skilled opponents, the traditional armor of ancient Chinese warriors during this early period consisted of individual metal scales fashioned together by leather to create a suit of loose-fitting armor that was flexible and well-adapted for close-range combat.

Therefore, ancient Chinese warrior armor was more sophisticated than what was worn by European knights centuries later during the so-called age of chivalry. In

Mulan's family and as mentioned, the suit of armor of her father had been considered a sacred relic that was considered something of rare beauty and it was something that was revered by the entire family, especially by his pretty daughter with dark eyes and long black hair.

From her early days and as noted, young Mulan had been attracted to these wartime relics of her father's service in defending the imperial court of the Khan against outside threats, which included the nomadic raiders from the north. To Mulan, the sight of her father's sword and suit of armor had sparked something deep inside her and for as long as she could remember, while fueling her admiration and interest for the martial arts.

Endurance of a Popular Folk Legacy

Unfortunately, there are no letters, diaries, or memoirs written by Mulan. She left nothing behind in written form but her legacy was faithfully told by generations of ancient Chinese in the oral tradition.

No evidence can be found that Mulan had been able to write or ever attempted to tell her tale in written form. As part of a nomadic society in the north, Mulan's early life had not centered around education that was considered unimportant compared to more pressing concerns of daily life. The young woman's formative education was gained from what she learned from living on the land and with the members of her family and clan, and it was one based on the difficult chores and traditional demands of daily survival in a harsh environment.

Therefore, Mulan's story has come to us solely from the ancient Chinese folk tradition and oral history that was first put into print by an anonymous Chinese writer (almost certainly a male writer) in the "The Ballad of Mulan" between the fourth and sixth centuries to reveal what had already existed for centuries in oral form to serve as the primary basis of the Mulan legend. As mentioned, it was first written in English for a western audience in the nineteenth century, after having existed for more than 1,000 years as a Chinese folk tale greatly beloved by the common people.

"The Ballad of Mulan" explained how her legend began on what seemed like just another average day: "Last night I saw the summons from the army, The Khan is mobilizing all his troops [and] The list of summoned men comes in twelve companies; Every copy lists my father's name" to serve in the army."

Because Mulan's father was aged and infirm and when the moment for decisive action descended upon her, Mulan boldly decided to wear his suit of armor, including helmet, to disguise herself as a male to serve as his surrogate to preserve not only his life, but also the family's honor.

She also possessed a set of well-worn weapons from her father's days of combat, but this was not enough. Therefore, according to "The Ballad of Mulan," she then secretly went to the different markets in town to mask her intent. At this time and at four separate markets to disguise her intention, Mulan discreetly purchased a horse, bridle, whip, and saddle for her military service that was destined to last for a dozen years.

As mentioned, recent archeology has proven that Amazons, the legendary female warriors immortalized by the ancient Greek writers who described their combat prowess in detail, were not just mythical entities and imaginary fabrications as long assumed by generations of western historians. Like the ancient observation that these bold warrior women of the steppes were the "equals of men," so these female fighters existed in the real world as in Mulan's case in northern China.

In fact and as emphasized by the ancient Greeks, some evidence has indicated that these even warrior women, especially leaders, deliberately gave up motherhood—just like Mulan during the war years that stretched for more than a decade for her—for the express purpose of serving as warriors to protect their people by focusing exclusively on the art of war.

Most important, western historians and scholars have long assumed that the source of warrior women exclusively lay in the tales from the overactive and fertile imaginations of the ancient male Greek writers, including leading historians like Herodotus, and that they were nothing more than old myths. But as noted, this was certainly not the case because of the ever-increasingly amount of evidence about the existence of warrior women in different cultures and in various lands around the globe that has continued to surface from the efforts of archeologists.

The fundamental truths of the notable example of Mulan, who hailed from north China during the Northern Wei Dynasty period, has fully demonstrated the fallacy of this Euro- and western-centric views of generations of western experts and historians, who had long denied the existence of ancient warrior women, especially the legendary Amazons. Like Mulan, these warrior women were not at all myths stemming from the fertile imaginations of male writers as long assumed, but real female fighters and warriors of flesh and blood.

In truth and although it cannot be determined, the inspiring example of female warriors was so prevalent throughout the course of ancient Chinese history centuries before Mulan's birth that the distinct possibility existed that she was partly influenced by the legendary stories and historical legacies of previous Chinese women warriors. The dramatic tales about these female fighters would have provided Mulan with a positive alternative image and view about how a female could do the impossible based on her resourcefulness and courage, after disguising herself as a male and the going to war.

Of course, this view is only speculative, because "The Ballad of Mulan" was so short, vague, and non-specific that exact details will never be known. Therefore, to better understand Mulan's amazing transformation and her motivations and how they developed and exactly why, the revealing examples of the lives of other warrior women, including in the West, have been utilized in this current book, because they have provided invaluable clues that help to explain some of the central mysteries that have long surrounded warrior women and their ordeals in wartime.

The rich stories and legends of Chinese warrior women, including dynamic female leaders and generals who orchestrated wartime strategies and who were highly-skilled in the martial arts like Mulan, have covered very nearly the entire span of Chinese history for more than 5,000 years. For instance, Fu Hao, who was also known as Lady Hao, was the first heroine of note in the annals of ancient Chinese history. During the thirteenth century B.C., Lady Hao led her army of male warriors to victory against the enemies of her people, while displaying a great deal of courage, skill, and ingenuity.

However and as mentioned, Fu Hao was only the first legendary female warrior of a lengthy list of Chinese heroines, who became cultural icons to the Chinese people for centuries. These courageous ancient Chinese women included revenge-seeking women fighters who were known as family avengers. These warrior women sought justice for the past wrongs that had been inflicted on their families. They fought with bravery and distinction against a host of enemies: bandits, rebels, raiders, and invaders, especially the so-called "barbarians."

Like so many other warrior women throughout the course of history, Mulan demonstrated that she could overcome all manner of adversity and obstacles—both within her society and against the enemies of her people—that were long thought to have been impossible for any woman to overcome with uncommon boldness and courage. All the while, Mulan overturned her society's most severe oppressions and restrictions that became formidable obstacles only because of her gender, while performing her duty to her family, Khan, and people with an extraordinary amount of skill in the arts of the warrior.

In a striking paradox and despite all of her remarkable qualities that became the stuff of legend for centuries, there is actually nothing at all unique and special in Mulan's years of faithful service because of one fundamental and undeniable fact: she was only one of a seemingly endless number of warrior women, including a long list of ancient heroines, who fought and served in the disguise of men throughout the course of history that has spanned continents, races, and cultures. This undeniable fact alone has made today's reality that Mulan has become a global icon that much more remarkable.

Indeed, Mulan has become the most beloved woman warrior heroine in the annals of ancient Chinese history, which has almost miraculously translated into her becoming the most famous of all ancient women warriors in the world today. Remarkably by the twenty-first century, the celebrated image and amazing story of Mulan and her battlefield heroics have transcended cultures, nations, and societies like no other female warriors who had also disguised themselves as males, while gaining international status like no other woman warrior in history.

Almost incredibly by the twenty-first century and thanks to the unprecedented power and global reach of the modern media, especially the Disney Company and its series of popular and highly-profitable films, this enduring ancient Chinese legend about a remarkable young Chinese woman has evolved into an international legend which has never lost its vast appeal in thousands of years.

Indeed, never before has a historical folk heroine, especially one whose origins have rested on an undated, short, and anonymous poem written more than 1,500 years ago, of an ancient people evolved into an international celebrity across the globe—perhaps the most remarkable aspect of all in regard to the Mulan legend and an entirely unprecedented one in world history. For example, Joan of Arc has long served as a western icon of a woman warrior heroine in the annals of western history, but her heroic legend and image were never embraced in the East like Mulan in the West.

After twelve years of arduous campaigning on behalf of her beloved homeland and family, Mulan returned home after the victory had been won. All the while, she had kept her precious secret from everyone. In the words of "The Ballad of Mulan" at the end of this short document from one of her male comrades: "We marched together for these twelve long years And absolutely had no clue that Mulan was a girl!" In the end, Mulan had served her family, people, Khan, and herself with rare distinction as a male warrior with considerable leadership and combat skills.

Chapter III

Historical Parallels in the West

Like in China, so the West has also possessed a hidden history of women warriors, who defied tradition and conventional norms of their respective societies by disguising themselves as men and going to war for God and country. Like Mulan, they possessed their own personal reasons that explained why they decided to fight while disguised as men and these explanations were varied to say the least.

For this reason, America has had plenty of its own Mulan's, both black and white, who served as women warriors in America's wars during the eighteenth and nineteenth centuries. In fact, America's women warriors have extended back to the days of the American Revolution, when Deborah Samson, or Sampson, of Massachusetts served against British forces during the fight for liberty. Deborah served in the ranks of the 4th Massachusetts Regiment of infantry, Continental Army, and she proved to have been a good soldier.

While most warrior women of America fought for the same reasons as the men in general, they also possessed their own unique set of motivations that were not unlike those of Mulan in ancient times. First and foremost, these adventurous women, who disguised themselves as men to fight on the battlefield, gained the freedom, mobility, and equality that could not have been acquired by them because of society's strict limitations on the female gender in almost every way possible.

Fortunately for these adventurous and bold women and as Mulan discovered by way of her own initiatives, the transformation from woman to man to the naked eye was so remarkably easy that it was unsuspected by men: merely changing from wearing traditional female dress to traditional male dress, which meant only putting on trousers for American warrior women during the eighteenth and nineteenth centuries. Of course, in Mulan's case, she donned her aged father's suit of armor that successfully hid her feminine form and metal helmet that hid her long hair that was pinned or tucked up under her helmet.

Most important in overall historical terms and regardless of what nation or time period, these defiant women warrior of considerable boldness have always crossed existing social, economic, class, racial, cultural, and national boundaries to become an unique historical phenomenon during periods of wartime over many centuries, as seen in Mulan's case, and for almost as long as humans have recorded their history.

In the process, these warrior women who disguised themselves as males to go to war systematically dismantled and utterly destroyed the simplistic negative female stereotypes long held dear by their respective societies, which kept women in lowly places and subservient to males for centuries.

In truth, the history of women in both the East and West has exhibited so many cases of dynamic and brave warrior women, including leaders, that it should no longer cause any surprise today among individuals of the general populace, because these female fighter should not be looked by people as anomalies or outliers in any way, shape, or form. After all and although mostly in disguise as males, female fighters around the world have always been in the mainstream of the human experience since time immemorial.

Fortunately, the fact that women have always donned male attire to go to war can no longer be doubted or denied and in most countries of the world. After all, the best documented examples of this phenomenon are most plentiful in the field of military endeavors and history during centuries of conflict around the world. As mentioned long before Mulan decided to go to war, Lady Hao, or Fu Hao, was the earliest heroine in Chinese history. And after the heroics of Lady Hao, China possessed a host of other female warrior women like Xun Guan, Lady Liang, and Lady Xian.

Lady Xian emerged as a Southern Yue leader and warrior of distinction. Among these legendary ancient Chinese women warriors were female members of the Yang family of the Song Dynasty who served as generals and led large numbers of male fighters while demonstrating their courage and skill in the heat of battle.

And Fu Hao, with sword and in a suit of armor, of the Shang Dynasty led thousands of men into battle. All of these legendary ancient Chinese women warriors, like Mulan, fundamentally conformed to core Confucian values and ethics, and these revered societal beliefs of a people's faith played a key role in motivating them to perform with skill during wartime.

However and as noted, female fighters and leaders were not just restricted to the annals of ancient Chinese history in the overall scope of Asian history. For example, the nation of Vietnam and their people have long embraced its own revered heroines who fought as males, especially the Trung sisters, who were known as "The Two Ladies Trung."

These dynamic warrior women and leaders of their people are remembered for having led the Vietnamese people in finally driving out of the hated Chinese invaders, who had descended in force upon their homeland from the north in 40 A.D., after nearly 250 years of occupation.

Significantly, thousands of North Vietnamese women of the North Vietnamese Army and South Vietnamese guerrilla forces fought against United States and South Vietnamese (ARVN) forces during the more than ten years of the Vietnam War. Exact figures are sketchy, but more than 10,000 Vietnamese women served in the lengthy war effort against the American invaders, including the dangerous mission of driving trucks along the heavily-bombed Ho Chi Minh Trail—actually a series of roads through the jungles and mountains that resulted in a highly-effective logistical support system—, which funneled thousands of men and tons of munitions from North

Vietnam to members (the guerillas) of the resistance effort in South Vietnam.

In part, these patriotic Vietnamese women fighters during the years of the Vietnam War were inspired by the heroics of the Trung sisters in their determined bid to hurl the Americans and their allies out of Vietnam, which proved successful by the end of April 1975 with the fall of Saigon.

Ironically, the cases of warrior women have been often documented in the context of freak occurrences throughout the course of history in the West, because the concept of female fighters was considered to have been deviant and anti-social behavior by males, who have most often provided the primary evidence about warrior women in their writings, because these emboldened females were worth noting partly since they threatened their patriarchal world.

Therefore, the female fighter was most noteworthy beyond the traditional reasons and explanations, including shock value because so many males could not imagine that the demonstrated equality of women warriors by these fighters was even possible on the field of strife, believing it was a hoax or fabrication.

Consequently, in overall historical terms and especially in modern times and until relatively recently, women warriors have been long ridiculed and dismissed as aberrations or freaks, whose behavior of fighting disguised as men ran directly contrary to the dictates of human nature and God's gender laws in male minds—some of the greatest of all male-based misconceptions and myths that have persisted to this day, especially in the West, in part because it has been primarily males who have written the historical record since ancient time.

But the legacies of female fighters have never died because they live today in the hearts and minds of the common people of their respective nations, especially in Asia. Therefore, the Trung sisters, who fought with distinction against the ancient Chinese invaders, have continued to be revered today across Vietnam as the nation's foremost heroines, just like Mulan in China, and revolutionary leaders.

Quite simply and contrary to what most male historians have written for an extended period of time, warrior women have been part of a lengthy popular tradition in both the East and West for centuries and as long as there has been recorded history. In consequence, there was absolutely nothing strange or unusual about warrior women and, hence, a lengthy list of dynamic heroines and leaders exist in the historical record, despite the many negative connotations and stereotypes about them that have continued to this day.

However in a striking paradox, the great interest in Mulan and other female warriors in general have stemmed from the ironic fact that the many examples of female warriors in the history of the United States have been ignored, overlooked, and forgotten until only recently and by the late twentieth century. Therefore, to the vast majority of people, women warriors have continued to be seen as something that has been a new development: hence, the subject of women warriors is a fascinating new field of study yet unexplored for the most part, representing a gold mine of historical information.

But as mentioned, history has fully demonstrated and proved that women warriors have been in the very mainstream of the human experience and from the beginning of recorded history: the antithesis of the male-based common stereotypes and assumptions about female fighters as aberrations and unusual occurrences in human history.

Throughout the course of American history and for hundreds of years, the United States has in fact had a good many of its own Mulan-like heroines and far more than has been generally recognized by generations of even leading scholars and historians. After decades of deep research into the historical record and as noted, this current author has written four volumes about the life of Cathy Williams of the post-Civil War period; five volumes about Harriet Tubman of the antebellum and Civil War period; and three volumes about Haitian Revolutionary Women of the Napoleonic period—all ground-breaking biographical series of remarkable black women that have promoted the true stories of revolutionary and warrior women and their remarkable experiences in the New World.

After all, Haitian revolutionary women, who were not disguised as males during their struggle for liberty in which everyone was needed in the ranks and large numbers of ex-slave females fought against the hated French, battling for more than a decade on behalf of the great dream of the first independent back republic, Haiti.

Across today's Haiti, these women wore French-style uniforms of revolutionary blue while battling for liberty and to ensure the death of slavery in this part of the Caribbean. After years of some of the bloodiest conflict ever seen in the New World, the Republic of Haiti finally became a reality on January 1, 1804, after the former slaves vanquished the forces under Napoleon Bonaparte, who had incorrectly envisioned as easy conquest of the French colony of St. Domingue (Haiti) in his racial arrogance and assumptions.

Long before Mulan became a global sensation, this current author began writing about the stories of remarkable warrior women decades ago, knowing that it was finally time for the lives of warrior women to be explored in greater detail because they represented a forgotten significant chapter of history that needed to be told.

Phillip Thomas Tucker's 2002 book *Cathy Williams, From Slave to Female Buffalo Soldier* was first published by Stackpole Books, Mechanicsburg, Pennsylvania, in 2002 to reveal the true story of Cathy Williams. Like Mulan, Cathy disguised herself as a male to serve as a soldier, who proudly wore the United States uniform of blue during nearly two years of service in a Buffalo Soldier regiment in the American West.

An ex-slave from Missouri, Williams faithfully served in a Buffalo Soldier regiment, the 38th United States Infantry, from 1866 to 1868 and proved, in her own words, to have been "a good soldier" from beginning to end. Williams even served on a difficult and demanding Apache campaign deep in the rugged mountains of New Mexico with her black comrades, including many former slaves, in arms. Like in the case of Mulan and the men who she served beside for years, the male soldiers who knew this remarkable former slave woman never realized that Private William Cathay (as her soldier name appears on her enlistment papers) was a female.

Significantly, Cathy Williams, who had been born in Jackson County, western Missouri, in the Missouri River country, was the first and only known black female to have served in the United States Army in the nineteenth century. After her nearly two years of service in the West from Missouri to New Mexico, she remained as a pioneer in the West.

Cathy settled in Trinidad, in Los Animas County southeast Colorado along the historic Santa Fe Trail, where she lived her life in a picturesque and rugged land in the mountains that she loved. However, Cathy Williams was a rarity in the historical record—the only known black woman who served as a Buffalo Soldier that became a forgotten chapter in black history until the publication of Tucker's groundbreaking books.

In regard to America's story, it was the Civil War which saw the widespread service of warrior women, disguised as men, from 1861-1865. Today because of the mounting body of historical evidence, it now has been generally accepted as fact that hundreds of women, in both Northern and Southern Armies, served during the Civil War disguised as men: a reality that would not have been believed by Americans only a few decades ago. In uniforms of blue and gray, these warrior women, who were mostly young and looked little different from the smooth-faced teenagers who served in Civil War armies, fought in some of the bloodiest battles of the war.

At least a dozen women disguised as men fought at the Battle of Shiloh, Tennessee, on April 6-7, 1862 and more than half a dozen warrior women were involved in the bloody showdown between the Army of the Potomac and Army of Northern Virginia at Antietam, Maryland, on September 17, 1862, and an unknown number of these fighting females were part of the contest at Gettysburg, Pennsylvania, where the largest and most decisive battle of the war raged from July 1 to July 3, 1863.

Some authors have briefly mentioned these examples of women warriors that have been almost always overlooked by generations of male historians as insignificant and meaningless. Unfortunately, at this time, there is an insufficient amount of evidence for books to be separately written by authors about the warrior women of Shiloh, the women combatants of Antietam, or the fighting women of Gettysburg. This situation might change in the future with the discovery of additional evidence about these warrior women, however.

Some articles, which are usually brief, about these remarkable women, who served in the armies of North and South, have appeared over the years in the United States, including one entitled "Confederate Amazons." But details and specifics have too often been lacking and warrior women have been treated as isolated examples rather than a widespread phenomenon in the mainstream of Civil War history.

DeAnne Blanton's and Lauren M. Cook's book entitled *They Fought Like Demons: Women Soldiers in the American Civil War,* has been the most definitive book to date about warrior women and it was very well received by the general public and the historical community. Most important, this book opened up the eyes of many people, and it will certainly ensure that future books will be written about this fascinating subject in future years.

This groundbreaking book by these two talented historians was published in 2002 by Louisiana State University Press in Baton Rouge, Louisiana. As authors Blanton and Cook emphasized in their introduction: "Our research produced evidence of about 250 women soldiers in the ranks of Union and Confederate armies" from 1861 to 1865. As mentioned, the emergence of the woman warrior has finally begun to enter the mainstream of thought and consciousness in America during the early part of the twenty-first century, thanks partly to this book's publication.

However, the central problem for any historian attempting to research the stories of warrior women during the four years of the Civil War has been the simple fact that enlisting in the army was done in secrecy and these women did not want to be known or discovered by males: a guarantee that they left few traces of their military service record, especially in regard to letters and diaries—an unfortunate situation quite unlike male soldiers who left behind an enormous amount of written material. However, ample evidence about these forgotten female fighters can be found after diligent searches in the historical record.

Even more, an increasing amount of evidence has revealed that the concept of women warriors has been long seen by males as so disgraceful and deviant that some male officials have deliberately eliminated primary evidence of their presence in the ranks, especially in regard to military service records during the prudish Victorian Era.

Consequently, for a host of reasons, the truth about the exact number of Civil War warrior women will never be known for this reason and a variety of others.

However, the total number of warrior women was much higher than the generally accepted figure of 400 female fighters who served in the Union and Confederate armies. In fact and because historians have finally taken a closer look at this long-ignored subject that has presented a host of new views and perspectives in a generally stale field of history because so much has been written about the Civil War over the years, some historians have estimated that thousands of American women, including many young females who were inspired by the legendary Joan of Arc, served during the four years of war. It is not known, but this might well be the truth in the humble opinion of this current historian from his own work in the fascinating field of study.

The peasant girl of rural France known as Joan of Arc became a heroic legend when she led the French people (Catholics) against the English (Protestants) invaders. Women from across America and on both sides during the Civil War disguised themselves as men and fought for their respective nations with the heroine Joan of Arc on their minds, serving as an inspirational example for generations.

For such reasons, the field of warrior women during the Civil War is still a largely untapped one at this late date of the second decade of the twenty-first century, inviting future generations of new scholars, both male and female, to conduct their own searches for forgotten warrior women to mine a rich field of study that is badly in need of thorough exploration at this late date: something that cannot be said about any other chapters of the field of Civil War historiography.

Chapter IV

Mulan Today

What are some of the forgotten factors that have explained why and how the legend of Mulan has seamlessly entered into the mainstream of American popularity and consciousness by the twenty-first century beyond the obvious factor of the films and global commercialism of the Disney Company? Interestingly, such basic questions have not been thoroughly explored at this late date.

However, one fundamental answer to this seldom asked question has been partly due to a young Chinese-American woman, who brought some of the most forgotten aspects of Chinese history and life into the American mainstream by her popular books for the first time in the last decade of the twentieth century, Iris Chang.

Unfortunately, however, Iris failed to live to see exactly how popular Mulan has become, dying tragically by her own hand when far too young and with many dreams still unfulfilled. Historian Iris Chang, a gifted Chinese-American historian and scholar, enlightened a new generation of Americans about the fascinating story of the Chinese people and the overall Chinese experience in America since the days of the "Old West," when large number of Chinese migrated to the west coast and primarily to California, before her tragic death at only age thirty-six.

Near the end of the twentieth century, Chang rose to prominence as America's best and only popular Chinese-American female historian in a field dominated almost exclusive by males. This remarkable young woman, who was sensitive, smart, and comparable to Mulan in a number of ways, achieved the rather remarkable goal of making Chinese history popular in the United States, where it became part of the mainstream because of her best sellers unlike at any previous other time. Iris' popularity was based on her wonderful skill in masterfully telling the story of the Chinese people on the mainland and the history of Chinese-Americans in America.

Born in Princeton, New Jersey, during a turbulent year for America in 1968, Iris Chang was also bestowed by her China-born mother with a Chinese name, Shun-Ru. This distinctive Chinese name meant pure and innocent that proved most appropriate and prophetic. The parents of Iris' mother, Ying-Ying Chang, escaped Nanking in 1937 before the horrors of one of the greatest atrocities of the Second World War—the grim subject that was destined to make Iris Chang world-famous in the late 1990s.

Most important, Iris' parents early instilled a love of China and its fascinating history to her daughter. She was also taught by her parents to have a pride in all things Chinese. Iris' mother, Ying-Ying who was an academic and a success story in her own right, passed the rich legacy of China's past to her daughter at her early age. Therefore, on American soil, the children of the Chang family not only grew up to become successful but also with a distinct sense of pride in the Chinese-American people and their culture and heritage.

For Iris Chang, it had all started with her early love of reading. As the daughter of two university professors, young Iris early developed a strong interest in reading, especially western fairy tales. This intense interest was naturally encouraged by her highly-educated parents, who duly informed Iris of many Chinese folk-tales from the distant past to fuel her interest and inquisitive nature, including the story of the young Chinese girl who became a legendary heroine, Mulan.

However, Iris also learned about American heroines, gaining a dual education that included both Eastern and Western heroines. Iris early became interested in Massachusetts-born Clara Barton, who rose to prominence during the Civil War, because of her courage and devoted care for wounded Union soldiers from the battlefields of America's bloodiest war. More important, Barton was the founder of the American Red Cross in 1881. Consequently, Iris was early drawn to the intriguing stories about strong women of great faith and bravery in the annals of both the western and the eastern history, especially Mulan, which left a significant and deep impression on her during her formative years.

While still at a young age, Iris Chang first rose to fame— not only national but also international—with the 1997 publication of her best seller book *The Rape of Nanking, The Forgotten Holocaust of World War II*. Coincidently, the publication of this best selling book came one year before the release of Disney's first *Mulan* film, the animated version, in 1998.

For the first time in a popular book of history released (1997) in the United States, Chang told the story of the forgotten holocaust of the Second World War that occurred in the city of Nanking, China, on the Yangtze River around four years before America's entry into the conflict. At this time, the world, especially the West, had forgotten about the unspeakable horrors inflicted on so many Chinese people, who were citizens and noncombatants, of Nanking by large numbers of the Japanese Imperial Army during one of the darkest chapters in modern history.

In December 1937 and January 1938, Japanese soldiers of the conquering Imperial Army were allowed by army leaders to rape and kill thousands (as many as 350,000) of Chinese citizens in a slaughter on a truly massive scale. Chang's fine book almost immediately became a *New York Times* best seller, turning into a blockbuster that shocked the United States and the world because of the awful truths that the book contained and revealed in full, including graphic photographs.

A gifted scholar and historian, Iris Chang was widely praised as a bright rising star in the historical community with only her second published book, *The Rape of Nanking*. In this timely work, she possessed courage by boldly telling the true story about the living nightmare of the slaughter at Nanking because of the sensitive political environment at the time, especially in regard to right-wing conservatives and politics in Japan. At this time and as today, Japan was a close ally to the United States, serving as a Far East democratic bulwark against Communist China.

Unfortunately for the young Chinese-American author, consequently, she received an inornate amount of criticism from the active front of extreme right-wing Japanese on the home island. These powerful nationalistic Japanese citizens were aggressive and politicized history deniers to preserve Japan's inflated image of virtue, despite the abundance of historical facts that were undeniable and revealed otherwise. They desperately wanted to silence the historical truths, as repeatedly emphasized by Iris during public speeches, of the full extent of Japan's crimes and atrocities so as not to tarnish the name of Japan and its pro-democratic image that had been marketed to the world since the Second World War's conclusion.

Despite the resistance and criticism to her book, Iris became an international celebrity and vocal spokeswoman and tireless activist for human rights, which fueled even more conservative Japanese resistance against her. In the words of her college professor mother, who felt a great deal of pride in seeing her daughter leading the way by telling the hard truths about history: "Some people told her that she was the Chinese Joan of Arc," because of her zeal and passion that fueled her activities that focused on undoing historical injustices in the face of strong opposition.

In the supreme compliment, some history-minded Chinese even "told Iris that she was Mulan, the legendary woman warrior who dressed in men's clothes and pretended to be her aged father's son, going into wars." Indeed, the heroic legacy of Mulan had played a role in having helped to make Iris not only a writer, but also a gifted historian of distinction and active political advocate for equal rights and justice. She also fought with passion for reparations from Japan to be paid to the Chinese victims, especially women, of the horrors that they had inflicted on the Chinese people during the Second World War, especially at Nanking.

Unfortunately, in continuing to pursue some extremely hard historical truths in Iris' typical bold and aggressive style, including intensive research for a future book on the Bataan Death March in April 1942 which told of almost unspeakable Japanese horrors inflicted upon prisoners after the surrender of the large American and Filipino garrison in the Philippines, touring a noted speaker around the world for women rights (thousands of Chinese women of Nanking were raped by Japanese soldiers and hundreds were killed), and the hectic schedule of her work had taken a severe personal toll on Chang.

Death threats from truth deniers also fueled Iris' increasing anxieties and fears because organized opposition to her had escalated and hardened by this time. The mounting pressures, paranoia, and depression induced by her ever-growing number of critics, especially the politically-powerful rape of Nanking deniers on both sides of the Pacific, ultimately played a large role in leading to Chang's suicide in 2004 to end the most promising of lives and futures.

Fortunately for us, Chang left behind an enduring legacy, however. She accomplished what once seemed impossible for a Chinese-American female by making Chinese history popular in America. For instance, Chang's final book *The Chinese in America* enlightened Americans about the overall Chinese experience and their forgotten contributions in the making of America.

But unfortunately, the life of America's leading Chinese-American historical scholar, who had still led a relatively balanced life as a mother and wife in California before her personal demons consumed her in a perfect storm, came to an abrupt end long before she reached her potential: a classic case of only the good die young.

In the end, Iris' mother, Ying-Ying Chang, wrote the best tribute to a remarkable young Chinese-American woman who died far too young and before she fulfilled her promise in the field of history: "In her short thirty-six years, she had inspired many, many people in the world with her noble spirit—her passion, dedication, sincerity, and determination—in preserving historical truth and in pursuing justice for the voiceless victims."

Ironically, in many ways, this enduring legacy left behind by Iris Chang was also very much the legacy of Mulan, whose inspirational story of female empowerment has continued to inspire large numbers of people around the world in the twenty-first century, including Iris when she had been growing up in the United States.

Like in the case of Iris Chang, the influence of Mulan and her heroic legacy can also be seen in the life of author Maxine Hong Kingston as revealed in her popular 1975 book *The Woman Warrior, Memoirs of a Girlhood Among Ghosts*. Kingston's work was still another best seller by a Chinese-American female author and one that possessed deep roots and connections to the legend of Mulan. In essence, Kingston basically told the story of the significant influence of Mulan in regard to his own life, which had been shaped by the legacy.

As she penned about her upbringing in America and the importance of Mulan's legacy in having molded her early life and that of her sisters and female relatives, who had found great inspiration in Mulan's story: "When we Chinese girls listened to the adults talking, we learned that we failed if we grew up to be but wives or slaves. We could be heroines, swordswomen. Even if she had to rage across all China, a swordswoman got even with anybody who hurt her family. Perhaps women were once so dangerous that they had to have their feet bound . . . My mother told others [stories] that followed swordswomen through woods and palaces for years. Night after night my mother would talk-story until we fell asleep. I couldn't tell where the stories left off and the dreams began, her voice the voice of the heroines in my sleep [and] After I grew up, I heard the chant of Fa Mu Lan, the girl who took her father's place in battle. Instantly, I remembered that as a child I had followed my mother about the house, the two of us singing about how Fa Mu Lan [the story of Mulan that had also been taught to Iris Chang by her mother] fought gloriously and returned alive from war to settle in the village. I had forgotten this chant that was once mine, given me by my mother, who may not have known its power to remind. She said I would grow up a wife and slave, but she taught me the song of the warrior woman, Fa Mu Lan. I would have to grow up a warrior woman."

Clearly, the inspirational influence of Mulan in the lives and formative development of young Chinese-American women in the United States, like Iris Chang and Maxine Hong Kingston, was a significant one and at an early age during a most formative period of their lives. A total of 16 years—less than a generation—existed between the unfortunate and untimely death of Iris Chang in 2004 and the release of the full-length Disney film *Mulan* in early September 2020: a development that partly indicated that Iris' success and best selling Chinese history-related books had helped to play a role in explaining Disney's success across the United States in promoting the story of Mulan and garnering millions of dollars in consequence.

Because young Chang evolved into one of America's leading historians—the first time development in the United States for a Chinese-American woman, who had been born in New Jersey, and especially at such a young age—who brought Chinese history into the American mainstream unlike any other author, the executives and marketers at Disney came to better understand the immense potential of the Mulan story. The Disney people more clearly realized how they could capitalize on the rich nuggets of Chinese history, especially in Mulan's fascinating story.

Clearly, in the legend of Mulan, Disney found a perfect and ideal subject, which had been long popular in Chinese folk history, to be fully exploited for global marketing, especially in the United States and aboard to the largest market with the most potential—the mainland of China. Indeed and as noted, as a young attractive woman of courage and faith who was motivated by love of family and the desire to protect her threatened native homeland from invaders, the subject of Mulan has proven to possess universal appeal across cultural, racial, and national lines, as fully recognized by Disney's marketers and Iris Chang at an early date.

Most important before the gifted author's untimely death by her own hand in California, the unbeatable spirit and fiery nature of Mulan had seemingly been resurrected in the form of Iris Chang, who had been early inspired by Mulan like countless other Chinese and Chinese-American women in Asia and America by the twenty-first century. Therefore, when people had told Iris that she was the modern Mulan, they were right on target, because Chang achieved, like Mulan, what was unthinkable for a young woman of Chinese descent to accomplish against the odds in a male-dominated world.

At the height of her popularity around the world after her book *The Rape of Nanking* was published in many languages, Iris Chang confronted a powerful and unified political opposition, while ignoring threats to her life and the increasing level of pressure and stress in her hectic activist life. Nevertheless, she continued to boldly demand that Japan officially apologize for its army's seemingly endless wartime atrocities that were committed by Japanese troops during the Second World War, when the aggressive conservatives of America's ally sought to silence the truth about what happened at Nanking and elsewhere across China during the Japanese invasion.

Most important, the key to an international audience's seemingly endless fascination with the story of Mulan has been the unconquerable and irrepressible spirit of this young Chinese woman with a big heart and good many combat skills for which she became legendary, while battling for the honor of her people and family against the foreign threat. The most enduring legacy of China's most famous female warrior was the fact that she demonstrated the importance of an individual boldly standing up and aspiring higher in life, while defying convention and tradition to do what she believed was right for her and her family. And in the process, Mulan made history and became an enduring legend second to none when it came to defiant warrior women, while ignoring the high personal cost and sacrifices.

The feisty spirit, heroism, and combat prowess of Mulan became legendary first in China and then around the world because she had nobly sacrificed her own desires for her family and people in the finest tradition of her society's Confucian ethical values, while achieving what everyone, especially males, believed to have been impossible for a young woman to accomplish on her own by way of her strength of mind, determination, and martial skills.

Chapter V

Modern Controversy

Completely unexpected by the top people at the Disney Company, the most recent film *Mulan* that was released on September 4, 2020 was greeted by a surprising backlash in both Asia and America. Recent political developments in China and Hong Kong have seemingly conspired to cause a severe backlash even before Disney's full-length feature film, which was made at the cost of $200 million, had been released, because of the repressive and anti-democratic actions of the Chinese Communist Government.

Most of all and from the beginning, the Disney Company attempted to appeal to the vast audience in China and thoroughly exploit this seemingly endless market—second only to the United States—to garner almost limitless revenues from a nation of nearly one and a half billion people in China.

Throughout the course of American history, including in regard to the longtime search of North American explorers and adventurers for the non-existent Northwest Passage to the Far East long before the United States was founded, generations of American businessmen and merchants had long dreamed of tapping into the full potential of the vast Chinese market and, of course, Disney was no different in this regard.

However, as mentioned, new political developments in both China and the West posed unexpected obstacles for Disney's ambitious pursuit of its most lucrative dream, which had once seemed so easily obtainable. The headlines of a September 11, 2020 article by Dan Gallagher in the *Wall Street Journal*, New York, New York, correctly emphasized the overall situation: *"Disney's 'Mulan' Experiment Gets Complicated."*

In fact, the use of the word "complicated" in this revealing headline might well have been an understatement under the circumstances. However, in truth, it was much more than just political developments around the world that caused a host of unforeseen problems for Disney by the time of the release of *Mulan* on September 4, 2020. First and foremost, most critics, especially in China, of the Mulan film have emphasized that Disney had been unfaithful to the historical facts and the true Mulan to an excessive degree.

The Disney Company has been repeatedly charged with having corrupted the authentic and original Mulan, transforming her from the real person of an ethnic Chinese woman to one who strongly adhered to state dictates, values, and expectations at the expense of her own self: the most heartfelt criticism of the 2020 *Mulan* film. And because Mulan has been depicted as having served the emperor and the central government, the Chinese Communist Government can now fully utilize their state-oriented version of the film for their own propagandistic purposes.

As noted, the top executives at Disney never anticipated the extent to this sharp backlash directed against the movie *Mulan* from multiple fronts, because of the relatively recent rise of current events and political developments, especially China's repression of ethnic minorities and harsh actions against pro-democracy activists and protestors in the city of Hong Kong. Hong Kong has been long controlled and ruled by China, representing a lucrative jewel of a city to the central government. In the media around the world, the new waves of oppression of ethnic minorities, especially the

Chinese Muslims, by the Chinese government have taken center stage to fuel greatest protests.

A *New York Times* article, entitled "Disney's 'Mulan' Criticized for Filming in Xinijiang," on September 8, 2020 emphasized how the new film "has become a lightning rod for criticism" against the Chinese government because of its aggressive crackdown on pro-democracy activities in Hong Kong and persecution of ethnic minorities in Xinijiang, northwestern China, where some of the 2020 Disney *Mulan* was filmed in 2018.

Less than a week later on September 14, 2020, the *New York Times* unleashed another journalistic salvo against the new Mulan film with the publication of still another scathing article entitled "Disney Wanted to Make a Splash in China with 'Mulan.' It Stumbled Instead." Indeed, large numbers of Chinese viewers stayed away from the film or came away in disappointment after viewing the film because of the widespread conclusion that Disney's *Mulan* was a drastic deviation from fundamental and authentic historical truths that have been long beloved by the Chinese people.

A Reuters article, written by Yanni Chow and Carol Mang, published on September 17, 2002 told of the problems that early emerged for the latest Disney film effort that had caught the company's executives completely by surprise.

Entitled "Disney's 'Mulan' Gets Cold Reception in boycott-leading Hong Kong," this article revealed how the leaders of the pro-democracy movement in Hong Kong, a Chinese ruled city long controlled in an autocratic manner, had orchestrated a boycott of the film, because of a long list of China's anti-rights actions and repressive abuses, especially against minorities in Xinjiang region in northwest China.

Here, in the northwest, the Chinese Communist Government had aggressively persecuted ethnic minorities, especially the Turkic Uighurs who were Chinese Muslims. An estimated one million Uighurs had been thrown into so-called reeducation camps, as emphasized by the Chinese Government, or concentration camps as viewed in the West. In truth and largely because of the Muslim faith, the persecuted Uighurs have been unlawfully rounded up from their homes across their ancestral homeland like cattle and kept for extended periods in what were internment camps with guard towers, armed guards, and barbed wire.

As mentioned, part of Disney's 2020 *Mulan* was filmed amid the mountains and deserts of Xinjiang—historically, the ancestral homeland of the Uighur people—, which added fuel to the boycott. Even more ironic, the historical Mulan was most likely an ethnic Chinese herself and not a member of China's majority ethnic group, the Han. Indeed, she was a member of a nomadic tribe and hailed from the northern region of China, which is the home of many ethnic groups, especially the Uighur Muslim people.

As mentioned, the historical Mulan was most likely a member of the Touba clan. The Touba clan was a distinctive ethnic group of a nomadic people of the Northern Wei Dynasty (386 to 534). Therefore, as fate would have it in a classic case of when historical facts and political developments have unexpected collided by 2020, the Chinese Communist Government's relentless and widespread persecution of ethnic minorities in the north has been especially ironic because Mulan was an ethnic Chinese from the north.

A September 16, 2020 article in the *Korea Herald* was more specific about the nature and the extent of the political opposition that had mounted against the new Disney film. This article revealed that the pro-democracy activists in South Korea began their boycott of *Mulan* even before the film's release in Korea. Part of the backlash centered on Disney's choice of cast for political reasons.

Unfortunately, the film's attractive lead actress, Liu Yifei, who played Mulan in the film had been active on her social media account in the past in a negative way, revealing anti-pro-democracy sentiments in her youthful innocence. In her post, she had emphasized strong support for the Chinese Government and the state police in their repressive attempts to crush the pro-democracy protests in Hong Kong by force.

Even more in a recent interview, Liu Yifei, who had been born in China but was partly raised in the United States to become a proud Chinese-American who has embraced both cultures and heritages, described herself as Asian instead of Chinese: an unexpectedly strong opinion that angered many Chinese because the actress had seemingly betrayed her early Chinese roots by not describing herself as Chinese.

In addition, the pro-democracy activists were angered that Disney had thanked a number of Chinese Communist state organizations, which had close connections to the persecution of the Chinese Muslims in the north, for their assistance in the making of the film in the credits at the end of *Mulan.* This fact was but one of a long list of criticisms about the new film that seemed to upset just about everyone for a wide variety of reasons.

Disney's political leanings and priorities also came into question. In the words of one pro-democracy activist: "It looks like the [Disney] company is trying to politicize the film." Indeed, the 2020 movie has portrayed Mulan going to war and fighting for the emperor of the main centralized government like most Chinese at the time, when in fact she served her nomadic community and the Khan of the Northern Wei Dynasty, who ruled her people—a non-Han Chinese ethnic group of the north.

Indeed, without ever realizing the extent of their mistakes in regard to the authentic historical record, the Disney Company had profoundly mixed politics with history in a most combustible fusion, especially in regard to current events: a situation which has revealed Disney's lack of sensitivity toward the sad plight of Chinese ethnic minorities, the extent of the central Communist government's repression, and the complexities of Chinese history to reveal an overly-simplistic narrative of Mulan, as portrayed in the 2020 film, in accordance to the self-serving agendas and priorities of the Chinese Communist Government.

Disney certainly deserved a large share of this sharp criticism because the sense of outrage had risen around the world about a wide variety of concerns. As noted, the 2020 movie *Mulan* was made by Disney with the assistance and cooperation of branches of the Chinese government that were connected in various ways with the persecution of ethnic minorities in the north.

Clearly, the factor of ethnicity in regard to the character of Mulan has become a bone of contention. As mentioned, the recent film has transformed Mulan into a member of the Chinese majority (or a Han who was a member of China's dominant ethnic group) who was loyal and fighting for the Chinese emperor (the main or central government) rather than her Khan, because she was actually a member of an ethnic minority of a nomadic clan in the north: basically, Disney's arrogant disregarding and "whitewashing" of the fundamental the truths of Chinese history with little regard to authenticity and historical realities, which proved unsettling to Chinese viewers of the film on the mainland.

Quite simply and as mentioned, Mulan was not a Han Chinese as portrayed in the 2020 film—the majority of people in China, then and today. All in all and as numerous critics charged, consequently, Disney succeeded in erasing Mulan's true ethnic (non-Han) identity in the overall process of minimizing the ethnic contributions of minorities in the north in the overall story of the making of China as a nation to conform with the Chinese

Government's deemphasis on ethnics, because of state agendas, including the persecution of minorities in the north, especially the Chinese Muslims.

In relative terms, this calculated elimination of ethnic roles and contributions in the course of China's history by the Communist state would be almost like American historians having deliberately ignored the important contributions of the Scotch-Irish in not only the American Revolution, but also in the "winning of the West": a key and inexcusable omission in the overall story of the making of America.

Therefore, in agreement with the Chinese government that has a strong agenda and platform to minimize the role of northern ethnic minorities in China's story that can partly justify its persecution of minorities in the north, Mulan was presented by Disney's 2020 movie as a member of the Han Chinese community without ethnic roots and with an unbridled loyalty to the emperor of the Han people and not her ethnic and nomadic people's Khan.

As mentioned, this was an inaccurate portrayal of Mulan that has proven upsetting to many people around the world, but especially in China: basically, an agenda-driven effort of the central Communist government's desire "to rewrite Chinese history in line with Chinese state-driven narratives" of China's rich past for its own self-serving purposes.

Protests by pro-democracy advocates against the persecution of minorities were held even in front of the Disney Company, South Korea branch, in the capital of Seoul. Like in many other publications across the United States and around the world, *Variety* magazine also launched an offensive of criticism against the most recent Disney film, which early fell under a barrage of criticism on multiple levels.

In a September 15, 2020 article, entitled "Why China Hates Disney's 'Mulan,' But it Has Nothing to Do with Politics," Rebecca Davis presented a hard-hitting case. She quoted one Chinese woman who maintained that Disney's 2020 effort resulted in the "the worst 'Mulan' in history"—a comment that was presented as a representative view and set the overall tone for this scathing article, while implying an universal consensus.

In fact and as revealed in this article by Davis, comments from citizens of China on the mainland were far more critical than from Americans, because of the vast cultural differences between East and West and since the Chinese people had grown up with the basic truths—overlooked or ignored by Disney—of the Mulan legend and had long held them close to the hearts.

In the words on one citizen from China, who especially objected to Disney's best effort to cash-in on the lucrative Chinese market with its 2020 film: "The Americans invited all the famous Chinese characters they could think of and piled together all the Chinese elements that they could find to create this car crash." As seen from this comment, even a certain amount of anger and a sense of outrage among a good many Chinese viewers had been generated by the Disney film.

Another Chinese reviewer emphasized much the same when it came to why so many Chinese people on the mainland strongly objected to the film: "It's full of Western stereotypes and conjectures about China and particularly ancient China." Most of all, Chinese viewers of the 2020 film objected to Disney's commercial fashioning of Mulan from a real historical person that they had grown to love since childhood days into a female superhero like Captain Marvel—the popular 2020 Superhero film distributed by Disney: a situation that drastically removed the main character and the film from historical realities in the all-out bid to create a blockbuster for the greatest profits.

In the end, the Disney Company, in one estimation, failed in its ambitious attempt "to bridge the cultural gap between the mainland [of China] and the West," which, to be fair to Disney, is very nearly an impossibility because of the extent of culture differences between East and West that could hardly have been greater. Most of all, this undeniable fact revealed that Disney had certainly needed more Chinese experts, historians, and consultants in the making of the final 2020 product in order to come much closer to historical truths and bridge this wide cultural gap that has existed for centuries between East and West, because of the film's lack of realism and the failure to remain true to the original story of Mulan and authentic Chinese history.

In this way by relying more on Chinese historians, experts, and scholars, the offensive Superhero Captain Marvel aspects of the 2020 *Mulan* film could have been early eliminated by Disney, because this was nothing more than part of the process of the film's thorough westernization in the company's bid to broaden the *Mulan's* appeal to a global market and reap as much profits as possible.

Even more and as revealed in this hard-hitting Rebecca Davis article and as mentioned, criticism of the film also centered on the choice of actress and former model, Liu

Yifei, who played Mulan. Of course, this mounting level of criticism toward the film's main actress was still another development that caught Disney by surprise.

While an attractive young Chinese-American woman with obvious talent on multiple levels, Yifei was very petite and delicate like the proverbial "China Doll" to the point that she is not fully believable in having performed arduous duty in multiple campaigns for years as a male fighting man.

Indeed, she obviously lacked the strength, body type, and durability for having endured years—a dozen years according to "The Ballad of Mulan"—of difficult campaigning, including in the mountains, and in many close combat situations to make the film seem less realistic and accurate.

Ironically, in this regard, the diminutive Yifei certainly needed the force of superpowers to make her notable achievements on the battlefield seem believable, because of her noticeable lack of physicality and strength. The executives of the Disney Company also thought so, because she was bestowed with supernatural powers to make the film unrealistic and cartoon-like.

Mulan's strong will alone could not have overcome the obvious physical limitations and liabilities of the slight and petite actress Yifei, whose overall delicateness could not be disguised in the film. Hence, the choice of actress virtually beckoned for the need of supernatural powers to make this petite, almost frail, young woman able to accomplish her feats on the battlefield.

As could be expected, this knowledgeable author of the *Variety* article emphasized the film's political aspects that have fueled a rising tide of criticism around the globe, because of what have been described as the Chinese Communist government's use of concentration camps for the Chinese Muslims: "The movie was filmed in the area in 2018 at the height of the campaign to put mostly Muslim ethnic Uighurs in interment camps [and] In the credits, the film even thanks government departments directly involved in the running of these camps."

In summary, Davis concluded how "Disney tried too hard for the Chinese audience and ends up alienating everyone." And this astute professor also observed how the movie ultimately "fizzles so badly that both American and Chinese viewers can see right through Disney's attempts to position the film as either authentic or empowering." As noted, this valid criticism additionally pointed to the dire need for the Disney Company to have used a greater number of leading Chinese experts and historians in the making of the film to eliminate errors and the many criticisms in China and the United States.

In addition, because of the highly-charged political climate of 2020 immediately before the November 4, 2020 election for the 47th president of the United States, the release of Disney's *Mulan* has also resulted in a greater political backlash across the United States. This largely politically-induced backlash that has focused on the support of human rights can be best seen in the words of journalist Rich Lowry of the *New York Post*, New York, New York. On September 8, 2020 and less than two months before the election to decide the president of the United States, Lowry penned how the most recent Disney Mulan movie "is the latest proof Hollywood has become a Chinese propaganda factory."

In an almost angry review in which the criticism of the Disney Company was exceptionally high in purely emotional terms, the author additionally wrote how: "Hollywood is accommodating a new era of McCarthyism—imposed this time by Red China—the [movie] studios have seamlessly absorbed Beijing's dictates into these questions. The most iconic American business is now literally, an agent of Chinese influence. The latest outrage is Disney's live-action remake of the animated 1998 movie 'Mulan' [that reflected] Hollywood's subordinate relationship to Beijing" and the leaders of the Chinese Communist Government.

In conclusion and in a common sentiment of many ultra-conservative Americans who have long voiced growing fears about the rapid economic and military rise of China into a major world power which has threatened the United States and its emergence as the American nation's chief rival in the world, Lowry emphasized how: "The upshot is that Hollywood is much more comfortable criticizing the United States than one of the most reprehensible regimes on the planet."

However and as noted, some of the greatest criticism was forthcoming from the people of China on the mainland. The 2020 film has been severely criticized in China for being too culturally and historically inaccurate and insensitive on multiple levels in the opinion of the Chinese people. Therefore, the film has failed to gain popularity in China as evident from the rising tide of criticism and the lack of financial proceeds at the box office.

As could be expected under the circumstances, *Mulan* has not garnered the great profits that Disney had expected in the vast Chinese market. Ironically, Disney failed in its effort to specially tailor the film for the lucrative Chinese market to maximize profits. The China market has been correctly deemed as virtually limitless in terms of revenues, ensuring that it became Disney's primary target.

Most of all and as noted, the 2020 *Mulan* film has been condemned by many Chinese viewers as being far too westernized and Americanized, which does not appeal to a culturally-sensitive and intelligent audience, which had grown-up having learned the intimate details of the heroic story of Mulan, especially on the mainland.

Therefore, Chinese audiences on the mainland obtained a distinctly non-China feel from watching the film to the point that certain elements were deemed offensive. Again, this is additional evidence that Disney had needed to rely more on Chinese experts in the film's making to ensure that such glaring mistakes were not made, when so much was at stake, especially massive profits.

Right on target in echoing the criticism of the Chinese people in general about the 2020 movie and as noted, one critic correctly ascertained that it was clear that the Disney Company's staff of producers, writers, and directors, who were mostly white and educated in the United States, failed to include the expert opinions and sage guidance of Chinese experts to avoid the mistake of a too-westernization of one of the most revered stories in all Chinese history.

Quite simply, Mulan's story cannot be realistically and authentically told with the required degree of historical accuracy and all of the necessary Chinese cultural nuances by westerners, despite their professionalism, experience, and college degrees like in regard to the Disney Company, because of their overall lack of intimate knowledge and nuanced expertise in regard to some of the most detailed aspects of Chinese history and the overall Chinese experience, especially in China.

To be fair to Disney, a faithful adherence to Chinese cultural values, historical nuances, and racial sensitivities of an iconic Chinese folk story has presented an extremely tall order, to say the say the least, for even the most experienced westerners, who possessed traditional western views and priorities from having been raised and educated in the West: the inevitable price that had to be paid by the Disney Company for their overly-ambitious attempt, not to mention arrogance, to appeal to audiences in both the West and the East.

As if this sharp backlash was not enough, the film *Mulan* also enraged members of the Chinese-American feminist community, because the movie portrayed Mulan's return to a traditional domestic role in the end: the so-called "happy ending," after having fought heroically for her people and family for more than a decade according to "The Ballad of Mulan."

Of course, there is considerable validity to this criticism because in regard to hardened wartime veterans and their difficult experiences in transitioning from wartime to peacetime environments from ancient to modern times. Indeed, after having engaged in a dozen years of warfare, there was little realistic chance that Mulan could have returned to her past ultra-submissive life in quiet domesticity and then enjoyed what has been portrayed by Disney as an extremely smooth transition—the ultimate submission of self in a return back to the harsh domestic servitude.

The extent of the backlash for the film was extraordinary because it came from so many directions and sources. In attempting to reach as many people as possible in the East and the West, consequently, it seemed almost as if the Disney Company had offended practically everyone by its ambitious 2020 release of a film that was meant to be all-inclusive to garner vast revenues. However, this savvy profit-based strategy of the Disney Company backfired to an amazing degree.

Two respected academics, Sin Wen Lau and Shih-Wen Sue Chen, wrote an article for *The Conversationalist* (internet) entitled "Disney's Mulan Tells Women to Know

Their Places." In their astute analysis, the two authors emphasized in the beginning how: "Disney's Mulan is a more conservative telling of an ancient story—and the place of women—than some historical Chinese renditions. While Mulan might claim to be a tale of female empowerment ultimately this film is about how women will only be rewarded if they know their place."

In conclusion, Sin Wen Lau and Shih-Wen Sue Chen lamented how: "Rather than being a story of female empowerment, Mulan promotes the idea that women must put male authority figures before themselves to achieve recognition."

By far, the hardest-hitting article that criticized Disney's 2020 *Mulan* was written by Kelly Hammond. She was a respected professor at the University of Arkansas. The article appeared on the internet in CNN Opinion section on September 17, 2020. The professor's article was entitled "Historian: I Watched 'Mulan' So You Don't Have To."

As emphasized by Professor Hammond, whose criticisms were harsh but valid for the most part: "With a timeless story as beloved as 'Mulan' it seemed Disney had backed a winning horse. But they managed not only to completely blunder the movie itself but also to wade into a political quagmire"—the mounting outrage and controversy over the central government's systematic persecution of ethnic minorities in north China, especially the Chinese Muslims, or Uighurs.

The financial failings of Mulan continued to be expounded by journalists throughout September. On September 30, 2020, Scott Mendleson published a *Forbes* article entitle "China Box Office: "'Mulan' is one of Disney's Worst-Performing Remakes." Mendleson's critical article was joined by a perfect avalanche of comparable articles.

By far and in summary, the most frequent problems and criticisms of the 2020 film that revealed the extreme dislike of Chinese audiences stemmed from the fact that Disney had bestowed Mulan with so many non-historical elements, including supernatural powers, which, of course, deviated from the historical and traditional story of Mulan, which was so well known to the Chinese people for centuries.

Indeed, a large part of the traditional and timeless appeal of the Mulan legend was the fact that she relied on her martial abilities, resourcefulness, and intelligence to transform herself by rising up on her own without the need of any outside power or magical forces for Mulan to succeed in accomplishing the impossible against the odds.

In truth and contrary to the superpower fantasy that has been so enthusiastically embraced by Disney when they failed to remain true to the historical facts of one of the most traditional stories in Chinese history, the historical Mulan had no assistance of any kind to have explained her dramatic rise to prominence during wartime in what was an amazing transformation for a young woman of courage and faith by her own willpower and efforts.

Again, unlike other ancient Chinese heroes and heroines, Mulan relied on no one else but herself to accomplish a great deal that was the moral lesson of the story to explain the primary source of its primary appeal: the very essence and core of the Mulan legend that explained why it has been so popular with the Chinese people for centuries.

By merely donning her father's suit of armor and hiding her long black hair under her war helmet, Mulan transformed herself and changed her identity into something revolutionary in wartime because of her determination to defend her beloved people and homeland and fight for her family's and family's honor: a diehard moral warrior woman who most of all loved her father, family, people, and homeland that she defended with her life in the finest Confucian ethical traditions of duty and sacrifice.

Contrary to the commercialized and sensationalized twentieth century image—the same one so eagerly embraced by Disney with massive profits in mind—of Mulan and as mentioned, she was not a Han Chinese woman who fought for the Chinese emperor. Instead, this remarkable young woman fought for her Kahn and her nomadic people, who were members of a distinctive ethnic minority, of the Northern Wei Dynasty in northern China.

In the greatest irony, the historical Mulan might well have been part of one of the same ethnic groups in northern China now discriminated against and persecuted by the Chinese Communist Government, including the systematic round-up and placement of tens of thousands of people from the ethnic minorities into internment camps for what the Chinese government has described as necessary for reeducation purposes: the so-called reeducation camps long so named and used by Communist governments, especially the Soviet Union in its longtime repression and exile of large numbers of its own citizens to Siberia, around the world from Asia to Europe.

Indeed, the so-called ancient northern "barbarians," as deemed by the Chinese government then and today, that consisted of ethnic minorities very likely included the historical Mulan, who might well have been viewed as an enemy of the Han-dominated state, which has evolved into an intolerant government, at some point.

Conclusion

But without the complexities of today's politics and the ultra-cultural and -historical sensitivities of the Chinese audience on the mainland, the enduring legend of Mulan, including the Disney Company's 2020 film, has presented a most uplifting and inspirational story that is timeless in its appeal to all people at all times.

Most importantly and as part of a lengthy and rich tradition of ancient female Chinese warriors who fought with courage in the defense of their homeland and people for over a period of 5,000 years, Mulan was a real woman of courage, quality, and character. And most significant, what she accomplished on her own required no sensationalism or marketing embellishments to appeal to a global audience or superhero fantasies to mythologize her achievements to tell the true story of this remarkable young woman.

Of course, the unfortunate excessive westernization and embellishments by the Disney Company of elevating

Mulan to superheroine status has developed for the express purpose of creating a commercialized product for mass appeal. However, this gross distortion resulted in a Mulan who was not historically authentic, because she was presented as if she had been nothing more than a popular comic book character, as fully realized by the disapproving Chinese people.

Clearly, as thoroughly revealed in the 2020 film, the systematic Disneyfication of Mulan in the crass pursuit of maximum profits has obscured the true story and fundamental historical truths.

Most of all, what was lost in the latest modern media version of Mulan was her cultural authenticity and humanness that had been held so dear to millions of Chinese for centuries: a simple and unfortunate case of whitewashing the historical record in Disney's aggressive pursuit of profits.

However, the true Mulan has not been denied all of her outstanding virtues as a legendary heroine by her transformation into a commercial product for the international market, because the core of her remarkable story has remained intact and secure. In the end, Mulan gained a rare measure of individualism, independence, and empowerment that she so desired by serving her people and land with distinction to become an enduring popular legend that will never die.

However, Disney's 2020 effort to make Mulan even more popular and legendary on a global basis was too extreme and over-the-top, coming at the expense of historical and cultural accuracy and these glaring defects were not lost of audiences in China and elsewhere around the world.

Most important, Mulan has still served today as not only an inspirational role model for Chinese woman, but also for women around the world—the secret to Mulan's timeless appeal to people, especially women, for thousands of years. Despite all of the modern shaping and reworking of Mulan's story by the profit-driven requirements of global commercialism from the original "The Ballad of Mulan" of ancient times by the forces of Americanization, globalization, and westernization, the historical Mulan has remained the same in the end in a most refreshing development. Even at this late date, consequently, Mulan has kept her purity and essence so beloved by the Chinese people.

Although what modern media, especially the Disney Company, created has been a mythical and nonhistorical Mulan because a wide variety of agendas, especially the process of tailoring Mulan for an international audience to maximize profits, and one that has been devoid of cultural and historical authenticity, she has continued to serve as an ideal, model, and icon to millions of people around the world to this day.

What has been long most admired about the historical Mulan was her authenticity and humanity which was the antithesis of the superheroine stereotype that Disney had incorrectly believed was the key to Mulan's greater popularity that could then be even more successfully exported to the international marketplace to reap greater financial dividends. However, this strategy was certainly not the case in 2002, proving to be a flat failure.

In truth and in hindsight in regard to recent developments after the release of the 2020 film Mulan in early September 2020, Disney only had to tell the true and authentic story without all of the unnecessary embellishments and excessive exaggerations that made Mulan seem much less human, especially when they bestowed her with supernatural powers in the superheroine tradition as seen in comic books and past popular movies, which have met with great commercial success in the past.

It was clear that the superheroine aspects of the main character were included expressly with profits in the minds of Disney executives at the expense of the historical Mulan and the true story that needed no exaggerations for presenting the finest possible portrayal of Mulan.

After all, the enduring legend of Mulan is all about what has always been the most important for any individual's personal success in life for aspiring individuals, both women and men, in either the ancient world or the modern world: a timeless story that has long fascinated and captured the imagination of millions of people around the world by providing an inspirational role model, especially for young women around the world, because she believed in herself and her abilities to do what others thought was impossible.

What will never be corrupted or lost has been the most ennobling of all human qualities of courage, individual empowerment, virtue, love of family and country, a distinct individuality, personal honor, sense of duty, loyalty, wisdom, remaining true to oneself, and self-respect, which have all been personified and celebrated in the story of Mulan. Mulan has embodied all of these sterling attributes and qualities to gain iconic status around the world unlike any other woman in the annals of history.

About the Author

PHILLIP THOMAS TUCKER, Ph.D., has won international acclaim on both sides of the Atlantic as today's leading "New Look" historian, who has authored a large number of "New Look" books of unique distinction. Throughout his lengthy career as a professional historian, he has long focused on a wide variety of unique aspects of the African American and Caribbean experience to reveal their full richness and complexities, while bestowing long-overdue recognition to forgotten men and women. Tucker's ground-breaking *Haitian Revolutionary Women Series* (3 volumes), *Harriet Tubman Series* (5 volumes). the *New Look Glory 54th Massachusetts Series* (4 volumes), and *Cathy Williams Series* (3 volumes) have continued the author's long-existing tradition of bestowing well-deserved recognition and praising the impressive achievements of remarkable African Americans, men and women, throughout the annals of history. One of America's most prolific and groundbreaking historians, Tucker has authored nearly 70 highly-original books to reveal long-ignored and silenced chapters of history, while correcting the historical record for the twenty-first century.

Bibliography

Blanton, DeAnne, and Cook, Lauren M. *They Fought Like Demons, Women Soldiers in the American Civil War*, (Baton Rouge: University of Louisiana Press, 2002).

Byers, Ann, *The Mongols, The Golden Horde and the Rise of Moscow*, (New York: Rosen Publishing, 2017).

Chang, Iris, *The Chinese in America, A Narrative History*, (New York: Penguin Books, 2004).

Chang, Iris, *The Rape of Nanking, The Forgotten Holocaust of World War II*, (New York: Basic Books, 2012)

Chang, Yanni, and Mang, Carol, "Disney's 'Mulan' Gets Cold Reception in Boycott-leading Hong Kong," Reuters, September 17, 2002.

Chang Ying-Ying, *The Woman Who Could Not Forget, Iris Change Before and Beyond The Rape of Nanking*, (New York: Pegasus Books, 2011).

CNN Opinion Section, internet.

Davis, William C., *Inventing Loreta Velasquez, Confederate Soldier Impersonator, Media Celebrity and Con Artist*, (Carbondale: Southern Illinois University Press, 2016).

Dong, Lan, *Mulan's Legend and Legacy in China and the United States*, (Philadelphia: Temple University Press, 2011).

Fraser, Antonia, *The Warrior Queens*, (New York: Alfred A. Knopf, 1989).

Greshko, Michael, "The Famous Viking Warrior was a Woman, DNA," National Geographic Online, May 28, 2020, internet.

Harriel, Shelby, *Behind the Rifle, Women Soldiers in Civil War Mississippi*, (Jackson: University Press of Mississippi, 2019).

Hook, Sidney, *The Hero in History, A Study in Limitation and Possibility*, (Boston: Beacon Press, 1943).

Kingston, Maxine Hong, *The Woman Warrior, Memoirs of a Girlhood Among Ghosts*, (New York: Vintage International, 1989).

Kwa, Shiamin and Idema, Wilt L., translated and introduction, *Mulan, Five Versions of a Classic Chinese Legend, with Related Texts,* (Indianapolis: Hackett Publishing Company, Inc., 2010).

Mayor, Adrienne, "The Real Amazons," *National Geographic History*, (May/June 2020).

McCarthy, Tyler, "Disney's 'Mulan' Criticized by Chinese Viewers for Depicting Culture, History in an Inauthentic way," Fox News, September 7, 2020.

New York Times, New York, New York.

The New York Post, New York, New York.

Nguyen, Hanh, *"'The Vietnam War,' How Vietnamese Women Saw Combat and Got in Other Harrowing Efforts*, IndieWire, September 25, 2017.

The Wall Street Journal, New York, New York.

Tucker, Phillip Thomas, *America's Female Buffalo Soldier, A New Look at the Life of Cathy Williams in History and Memory*, (Portland: PublishNation, 2017).

Tucker, Phillip Thomas, *Cathy Williams, From Slave to Female Buffalo Soldier*, (Mechanicsburg: Stackpole Books, 2002).

Tucker, Phillip Thomas, *Harriet Tubman's Revenge and a New Birth of Freedom: Guiding the Combahee River Raid in a Holy War of Liberation*, (Portland: PublishNation, 2109)

Tucker, Phillip Thomas, *Nanny's War to Destroy Slavery*, (Portland: PublishNation, 2018)

Variety, New York, New York.

Washington Post, Washington, D.C.

Wheelwright, Julie, *Amazons and Military Maids, Women Who Dressed as Men in Pursuit of Life, Liberty, and the Pursuit of Happiness,* (London: Pandora Press, 1990).